WOMEN FILMMAKERS OF THE AFRICAN AND ASIAN DIASPORA

WOMEN FILMMAKERS OF THE AFRICAN AND ASIAN DIASPORA

DECOLONIZING THE GAZE, LOCATING SUBJECTIVITY

GWENDOLYN AUDREY FOSTER

SOUTHERN ILLINOIS UNIVERSITY PRESS

CARBONDALE AND EDWARDSVILLE

Library of Congress Cataloging-in-Publication Data
Foster, Gwendolyn Audrey.
Women filmmakers of the African and Asian diaspora : decolonizing the gaze, locating
subjectivity / Gwendolyn Audrey Foster.
p. cm.
Includes bibliographical references and index.
1. Afro-American women motion picture producers and directors. 2. Women motion
picture producers and directors—Asia. I. Title.
PN1998.2.F672 1997
791.43′0233′092273—dc20   96-27635
ISBN 0-8093-2119-X (cloth : alk. paper). — ISBN 0-8093-2120-3 (pbk. : alk. paper) CIP

❖   FOR WHEELER   ❖

CONTENTS

ILLUSTRATIONS

ACKNOWLEDGMENTS

IN CREATING THE text of *Women Filmmakers of the African and Asian Diaspora: Decolonizing the Gaze, Locating Subjectivity*, I am deeply indebted to the work of many writers and filmmakers, including Bill Nichols, N. Frank Ukadike, Mbye Cham, Claire Andrade Watkins, Teshome Gabriel, Kobena Mercer, David Nicholson, Clyde Taylor, Mark Reid, Homi K. Bhabha, bell hooks, Renato Rosaldo, Chandra Mohanty, Jacqueline Bobo, Gloria Gibson, Trinh T. Minh-ha, Pratibha Parmar, Zeinabu irene Davis, Julie Dash, Ngozi Onwurah, Safi Faye, Gayatri Chakravorty Spivak, B. Ruby Rich, Amy Taubin, Michele Wallace, Toni Cade Bambara, Greg Tate, Ana López, Judith Mayne, Manthia Diawara, and Teresa de Lauretis.

Sincere thanks as well to Linda Ray Pratt, chair of the Department of English of the University of Nebraska, Lincoln, for her continuing support of my work. I am also grateful for the assistance of Brian Zillig and the staff of the Interlibrary Loan Service, Love Library, at the University of Nebraska, Lincoln, for their help in securing many reference materials, and to the staff of Women Make Movies, Inc., who made available research materials and still photographs on many of the artists discussed here, so that I might better discuss their lives and careers. I also owe a debt of gratitude to the staff of the Black Film Archive at Indiana University for their assistance. Finally, I sincerely thank Wheeler Winston Dixon, Oyekan Owomoyela, Maureen Honey, Joy Ritchie, Kate Ronald, Alpana Knippling, and Tony Williams for their discussions and advice on this volume.

WOMEN FILMMAKERS OF THE AFRICAN
AND ASIAN DIASPORA

INTRODUCTION

DECOLONIZATION OF THE "gaze," and the re/construction of sites of filmic diasporic subjectivity is particularly difficult because of the persistence of white hegemonic Hollywood constructions of spectatorship, ownership, and the creative and distribution aspects of filmmaking. Many critics have demonstrated how films of the African diaspora and the Asian diaspora are effectively marginalized by a predominately white Western distribution system. Although these cinematic traditions address widely disparate concerns, both African and Asian diasporic cinemas share a project of reclaiming and imaging subjectivity and decolonizing the gaze. This seems to be particularly true in the case of the work of women filmmakers of the African and Asian diasporas. Despite such obstacles, women filmmakers of the African and Asian diaspora have been articulating and reconstructing cinematic subjectivity since even the earliest days of cinema, when **Eloice Gist**, an African-American contemporary of pioneering African-American filmmaker Oscar Micheaux, was already bringing her own vision to the screen. Gist wrote, directed, and self-distributed revivalist spiritual films that she exhibited as a traveling evangelist in the South during the Great Depression. Gist's films include *Hell Bound Train* and *Verdict Not Guilty*; in addition to her travels in other states, Gist toured with the films in and around Washington, D.C., and as far north as New York City, under the sponsorship of the NAACP. Gloria Gibson and other film scholars are currently at work unearthing these films from various private and public archives.

Other African-American women filmmakers active during the early part of the twentieth century include **Lita Lawrence**, who directed the feature film *Motherhood: Life's Greatest Miracle* in 1927, as well as **Eslanda Goode Robeson** and **Alice B. Russell**, who worked with Oscar Micheaux. In addition, recent scholarship has unearthed the fact that **Zora Neal Hurston** filmed a series of recently rediscovered ethnographic short films in the 1920s. Despite the Hollywood publicity machine's insistence that each new Black woman director is the "first Black woman director," Black women and women of the African, Asian, and Latin American diasporas have been persistently active, both in Hollywood and independent filmmaking, especially in the last twenty years. Writing on the "cinematic sisterhood" of Black women directors, Greg Tate, of *The Village Voice* observed:

> Black film can be a political, spiritual, and historicizing power base for us as well as an aesthetic and economic one. Quiet as it's kept, if you want to find a group of Black filmmakers kicking that kind of science, you got to go to the sisters. Matter of fact, after interviewing sisters for this piece, I stepped back feeling like a lot of the young brothers out here on the Black film mission ain't about nothing but some self-serving, self-aggrandizing, macho-posturing-ass bullshit. Yo, what do a brother know? If we're talking about visionary narratives and subject matter, and filmmakers grounded in daily struggles against sexism, white supremacy, and professional marginalization, the sisters are the ones I hear taking no shorts and talking no sellout. . . . They're more about solidarity. There's not one woman I talked to who didn't take the opportunity to pump up three or four of her sister filmmakers. (1991, 77)

The erasure of black women's filmmaking and the continued denial of the presence of a loosely knit diaspora of Black women filmmaking sisterhood is consistent with the racist colonialization of Black female subjectivity and Black women's images stories, identities, and spectatorship. African-American women and people of color are eager for images of multicultural female subjectivity that are constructed from a Black female point of view. This desire is nothing new, for as Jacqueline Bobo comments in her book *Black Women as Cultural Readers*, Black women and other women of color have always been active as oppositional spectators and as cultural producers of artwork that takes an "oppositional stance" (136). As Bobo sees it:

> Within the last several decades black women have effectively written themselves back into history; they have retrieved their collective past for sustenance and encouragement for present-day protest movements. . . . .Even as the image of docile, obsequious black women remains a popular construction for mainstream cultural producers, the history of black women's activism shows that black women are not the acquiescent martyrs of popular imagination but women who effectively meet the repressive challenges of mainstream society. (36–37)

Women filmmakers of the African diaspora display a heterogeneity of forms. Though they share a cinematic sisterhood dedicated to finding a language and space for subjectivity, they certainly shouldn't be constructed as a homogeneic or essentialist, overdetermined group. Instead, theirs is a scopic space of "post Negritude," as it is defined by film critic Mark Reid:

Post Negritude refers to any moment when members of the black community, through their literature, art, and politics, recognize that black culture is concretely an open-ended, creative dialogue of subcultures, of insiders and outsiders, of diverse factions. (1993, 113)

This book is a critical study of six women directors of color, each of whom represents a unique, yet heterogeneous body of film work. All of the filmmakers studied here are aware of the politics of post-colonialism, and all take their own approaches to diasporic cinema. These women challenge dominant cinema, which is predominately white, Eurocentric, and male dominated. Nevertheless, they resist and disrupt racism, sexism, and homophobia, which are ever-present in most world cinema. "Feminist theory rooted in an ahistorical psychoanalytic framework that privileges sexual difference actively suppresses recognition of race," writes bell hooks, "reenacting and mirroring the erasure of black womanhood that occurs in films" (1992, 123). If, as hooks states, some feminist theorists have been guilty of erasing black women as spectators, they have been equally guilty of ignoring black and Asian women as cultural artists. More importantly, film critics in mass media generally ignore the independent films of African-American and Asian-American women, while they champion the films of Spike Lee, Robert Townsend, Matty Rich, and other African-American and Asian American men. But many independent women filmmakers are actively seeking to change these disparities.

In creating this book, and in choosing the women directors included in this volume, I have been highly aware of the problematic nature of diasporic studies. There are many other women directors working within the African and Asian diasporas, and I could not possibly include all of the filmmakers I wished to. Nevertheless, this volume covers many of the major figures working within this wide, diverse, and oppositional cinema/video practice, women whose films have been, to some extent, marginalized by the distribution system of the dominant Hollywood cinema. My methodology springs from an interest in and dedication to the study of difference. Linda Gordon reminds us of "what is being avoided" when Western critics speak of one category of (racial and gendered) difference: "the denial of the possibility of human subjectivity . . . belittles the search for shared meanings of womanhood . . . " (105). Difference study, Gordon concludes, can often result in an environment that is "constricting, even paralyzing" (106) and has a "chilling effect on the struggle to recognize others and hence to end the categorization 'other' " (107). Filmmaker and cultural critic Trinh T. Minh-ha underscores the problematics of studies of difference and the "other" with the statement, "The idea that there is a hidden truth in the other's culture that needs the joint effort of the outsider and the insider to be fully unveiled is highly misleading" (1992, 238).

Even as I call into practice a decentered position, I am aware that I must not "silence by a telescoping act of interpretation the multiple and specific voices" (Smith and Watson, xxviii) of women of the African and Asian diaspora. Critics such as Elizabeth Abel argue that "If we produce our readings cautiously and locate them in self-conscious and self-critical relation, [we are] thereby expanding the possibilities of dialogue across as well as about racial boundaries" (498). Gayatri Spivak locates the need for a speaking "feminist internationalist," granting, however, the ironies involved, "when we mobilize that secret ontic intimate knowledge, we lose it, but I see no other way" (1992, 803). In Spivak's schema, it is the Western critic who becomes an Other and who is, in effect, problematized.

Approaches to decolonizing my own critical apparatus is by no means a simple or straightforward task. It is an area fraught with issues of power relationships that cut across disciplines and deconstructs notions of identity. Critical discourse may seem to be treading its wheels mired in a muddy impasse, one which is well characterized by Spivak, who recognized, in 1987, that "the radical intellectual in the West is either caught in a deliberate choice of subalternity, granting to the oppressed either that very expressive subjectivity which s/he criticizes or, instead, a total unrepresentability" (209). Unfortunately, many women filmmakers have had their work ignored and/or poorly distributed, to some extent I think because of this critical crisis of representation. One response has been the formation of independent filmmaking collectives such as The Sankofa Film and Video Collective. Sankofa, for example, responded to the silencing of neocolonial British Black culture with their film *The Passion of Remembrance* (1986). Maureen Blackwood and other members of the collective, told an interviewer "We couldn't deny our history, our knowledge" (Jackson and Rasenberger 23). Describing the film community of "apprehension" in England as a "crisis," their remarks could easily be applied to the academic environment. The collective "decided to use fiction because it opened up a space to fantasize about possibilities, even though we don't have answers" (Jackson and Rasenberger 23).

The feminist critical community can learn from the example of this collective group and perhaps learn to pose more questions than answers. In doing so, perhaps we can adopt Linda Gordon's suggested strategy of "transformation of the difference slogan into a more relational, power-conscious, and subversive set of analytical premises and questions" (107). The task of cultural critic is not only centrally consumed with questioning "the politics of identity as given, but to show how all representations are constructed, for what purpose, by whom, and with what compliments" (Said 314). Studying the international films of independent women directors should be one of the main tenets of such a task.

In addition, the inherent hegemonic presumptions of reading texts from "Other" worlds have been based on the notions of fixed identity and fixed historicity. As Yuejin Wang demonstrates, when "historical flux is acknowledged, the notion of cultural identity loses its fixity," and "the very paradigm of the self versus Other has to be reversed" (32). For Homi Bhabha, the latter is by no means simple, or even operational, for "the term 'critical theory,' often untheorized and unargued, was definitely the Other" (1989, 111). Bhabha's comments, concerning an academic film conference, and the Western logocentricism of criticism, reiterate common problematics of film criticism:

> What is at stake in the naming of critical theory as "Western"? It is obviously, a designation of institutional power and ideological Eurocentricity. Critical theory often engages with Third World texts within the familiar traditions and conditions of colonial anthropology either to "universalise" their meaning within its own cultural and academic discourse, or to sharpen its internal critique of the Western logocentric sign, the idealist "subject," or indeed the illusions and delusions of civil society. (1989, 123)

Critical approaches to the cinema of women of color, if one can even speak of such a category, is then located on the grid of intelligibility that is contextualized in inherent power struggles of meaning and sign ownership. Even poststructural and postmodern approaches have been recently characterized as "metanarratives" that "threaten to treat ex-colonial peoples as bounded units, cut off from their historical contexts" (Coronil 103). If "the concept 'woman' effaces the difference between women in specific socio-historical contexts, between women defined precisely as historical subjects rather than *a* psychic subject" (hooks 1992, 124), how can one speak of "women's" cinema, much less "diasporic" cinema? The use of the terms "African diaspora" and "Asian diaspora" should not be taken to imply some utopic definition of essentialist, totalized groups or identities. Indeed, many of the women filmmakers in this study fall into both categories, thus demonstrating the impossibility of rigid categorization. As Trinh T. Minh-ha notes, "The claim of identity is often a strategic claim" (1992, 157). Here I hope to use the claim of identity to respect difference while I do wish to emphasize my awareness of the problematics of identity within postcolonial discourse.

The critical testimony and the films of women filmmakers such as Julie Dash exemplify sites in which one can locate the speaking subject of a deobjectified post-colonial tongue/camera. As a critic, I assume the subject position of the listener, rather than the dominant position of the gazer/criticizer, in studying the films of women of the diaspora. As Fernando Coronil suggests, perhaps this practice may foster decolonialization "outside and within academia" (106). For Suleri, the critical repositioning of the "racial body in the absence of historical context" is a "hidden and unnecessary desire to resuscitate the 'self' " (762). Suleri cautions against the dangers of divisive binarisms within feminist discourse, maintaining that the "category" of "woman of color" is as nascent and politically charged as "woman" herself. Judith Mayne, for example, locates a discomfort within the category of Third World Women's cinema, as it lays a "burden of the demonstration of cultural difference" (1990, 222), on the filmmaker. Nevertheless, Mayne points out that it is perhaps equally problematic to categorize the films of women of color in a tradition of "women's cinema" as this risks "the flattening out of difference" (1990, 221).

Feminist criticism must continue to allow for violently opposing viewpoints, because, as Chandra Talpade Mohanty stresses, "however sophisticated or problematical its use as an explanatory construct, colonization almost invariably implies a relation of structural domination, and a suppression—often violent—of the heterogeneity of the subject(s) in question" (52). It would hardly be useful or prescient to suppress postmodern approaches of diasporic women's cinema, especially to position a monologic feminist definition of self. That the debate has been so rigorous reflects a continuing interest in defining the self, which, as Julie Watson and Sidonie Smith note, is central to Western meaning: "the politics of this 'I' have been the politics of centripetal consolidation and centrifugal domination" (xvii). The outlaw cinema of Pratibha Parmar, for example, and the work of many diasporic women filmmakers is involved in a struggle similar to that of the postcolonial woman writer. As " 'illegitimate' speakers [they] have a way of exposing the instability of forms" (Smith and Watson xx).

The crisis of representation of African-Americans, Asian-Americans, and women of color in academic discourse as a multitiered, politically charged agenda. Toni Morrison, however, discourages "totalizing approaches to African-American scholarship which has no drive other than the exchange of domination—dominant Eurocentric scholarship replaced by dominant Afrocentric scholarship" (8). More interesting to Morrison, and perhaps more pertinent is the underlying question, "what makes intellectual domination possible, how knowledge is transformed from invasion and conquest to revelation and choice; what ignites and informs the literary imagination, and what forces help establish the parameters of criticism" (Morrison 8). Speaking for/about an/other will and should continue to be fraught with difficulties, enigmas, crises in representation, and fractures, because, as R. C. Davis writes:

> The power to control the positions of speech and of what can be said—as Edward W. Said has said about authority in general and as Cixous and Spivak demonstrate about patriarchal authority specifically—"must be analyzed" before any effective social critique can take place. (41)

Feminists have much to learn from women of the diaspora. We can take responsibility, like Diane Bell, by not speaking for the Other, but instead "provide a basis on which cross-cultural understanding may be built, to locate issues of gender and race within a wider perspective, to offer an analysis of social change" (23). In adapting ourselves to the task, we might well listen to the voice of Trinh T. Minh-ha, who writes, "The precarious line we walk on is one that allows us to challenge the West as the authoritative subject of feminist knowledge, while also resisting the terms of binarist discourse that would concede feminism to the West all over again" (1992, 153).

My main aim throughout this book is to locate the strategies that women filmmakers of the diaspora are using to decolonize the gaze and to ground their films in subjectivity. In Chapter 2, I locate **Zeinabu irene Davis** as one of a growing number of independent black women filmmakers who are actively constructing "an oppositional gaze," a term bell hooks uses to describe films that look through/at African-American female experiences through a Black lens. Zeinabu films seek to reclaim Black female subjectivity through poetic (re)constructions of time, the body, and an exploration of spatial configfurations. In Chapter 3, I consider the work of filmmaker Black British filmmaker **Ngozi Onwurah**, who, like Zeinabu Davis, takes on the issues of time and space in her work which embraces heterogeneity and multiple sites of subjectivity. Onwurah consistently navigates and challenges the limits of narrative and ethnographic cinema by insisting that the body is the central landscape of an anti- imperialist cinematic discourse.

In Chapter 4, I analyze the films of African-American **Julie Dash**, whose *Daughters of the Dust* challenges Hollywood narrative techniques which typically ignore African-American history, particularly Black women's history. It also reflects how mainstream documentary and ethnographic approaches tend to objectify the Black subject as object. Like Davis and Onwurah, Dash is noted for her reconsideration of time and space, and her celebration of the black body and African-American cultural diversity. In Chapter 5, I discuss the films and videos of **Pratibha Parmar**, which center around issues of representation, identity, cultural displacement, homosexuality, and racial identity. The Kenyan-born Anglo-Asian British filmmaker began working in film and video in the 1980s. In Parmar's films she locates woman as speaking subject, gazing subject, interrogating corporeal performative subject who owns spatiality in an arena that once depended upon her invisibility, her silence, and the suppression of her subjectivity. Chapter 6 is a study of **Trinh T. Minh-ha**, who revolutionized documentary filmmaking with her poststructuralist avant-garde films that displace the voyeuristic gaze of the ethnographic documentary filmmaker. Theorist, filmmaker, and composer, Trinh T. Minh-ha is one of the most respected postcolonial artists of the late twentieth century. Born in Vietnam, Trinh T. Minh-ha came to the United States in 1970. After graduate school, Trinh T. Minh-ha studied in Senegal and Dakar. Her work as an ethnographer led her to question the notions of ethnography. She argues that ethnographic filmmaking did not objectively represent the Third World Subject, and she questioned the validity of "objective truth." In Chapter 7, I evaluate the work of **Mira Nair**, an internationally recognized Black Indian woman filmmaker of the Asian diaspora. Interracial identity is the central theme in many of the films of Mira Nair, who has emerged as a pioneer of the diasporic filmmaking community. Nair's work in documentary and narrative film is both challenging and celebratory. Born in Bhubaneswar, Orissa, India in 1957, Nair came to the United States to study at Harvard University after working as an actress in New Delhi. Nair has a formidable career that began with her work in documentary and ethnography and culminated in the more recent productions of independent narrative films such as *Mississippi Masala* and *The Perez Family*.

Chapter 8, "Other Voices," considers the work of a broad range of women filmmakers of the Asian and African diasporas, including African-American lesbian director **Michelle Parkerson**, who is widely respected in the African-American and gay/lesbian/bisexual communities for her films that celebrate African-American and queer subjectivity. Other African-American women directors included in this chapter include **Kathleen Collins, Jackie Shearer, Ayoka Chenzira, Camille Billops, Barbara McCullough, Alile Sharon Larkin, Dawn Suggs, Cheryl Dunye, Leslie Harris** and **Darnell Martin**. Directors of the Pan-African diaspora found here include **Martina Attile** and **Maureen**

Blackwood, both of the Black British Sankofa collective, and **Maria Novaro**, who is a fairly well known Mexican filmmaker, and Caribbean filmmaker **Euzhan Palcy**, who is best known for *A Dry White Season*, one of the first films to deal with apartheid in South Africa. I have also included sections on Aboriginal and Native-American women directors such as **Merata Mita, Tracey Moffatt, and Alanis Obomsawin**. In defining the scope of this study, I have used the term "the diaspora" in the widest sense in order to include women filmmakers of the African and Asian diaspora including **Gurinder Chadha**, director of *Bhaji at the Beach*; **Christine Choy**, director of *Who Killed Vincent Chin?* and **Ann Hui**, director of *Boat People*. I also briefly consider African directors **Sarah Maldoror** and **Safi Faye**. The reader is directed to the works cited at the conclusion of this volume for additional resource materials on these talented artists.

In all of its many manifestations, the women filmmakers of the diaspora have contributed a unique vision of the world and its inhabitants for viewers who are, perhaps, more accustomed to participating in the vision offered by the dominant cultural machine of the Hollywood cinema. Working outside the traditional image-making system, these women have created powerful and moving images that tell the stories of their shared existences together, and bind the respective visions of their works to the consciousness of their projective audiences. These films all begin the very important work of decolonizing the gaze, and articulating fresh and flexible diasporic modes of subjectivity in the cinema.

❖ 2 ❖

ZEINABU IRENE DAVIS
"Constructing an oppositional gaze"

TONI CADE BAMBARA comments that the cultural work of Black independent cinema includes the radical "fashioning of a deliberate diasporic aesthetic" (128). Bambara reads the work of African-American filmmaker Zeinabu irene Davis through the prism of a diasporic aesthetic that is part of a continuum of the works of independent Black filmmakers such as Julie Dash. An aesthetic pull toward an "oppositional gaze" as described by bell hooks (1992, 115) remakes constructions of blackness and femaleness (as viewed through the traditions of the colonial white gaze) and transforms these notions into performances of a heterogeneous diasporic gaze of Black female subjectivity (rather than objectivity). Zeinabu irene Davis' *Cycles* (1989) is but one example of the films of the diaspora that seeks to reclaim black female subjectivity through poetic (re)constructions of time, the body (particularly menstruation), and the cultural work of the African-American woman.

Cycles is a short but highly important work of diasporic cinema. Zeinabu said of the film, "There was something going on in that film that really cut the nerve. *Cycles* is a very dense film, but I think there was something that I hit upon that I would like to further explore in terms of delineating a language, a visual language, that specifically reflects the lives of women" (Filemyr 9). The "black womanist subjectivity" (Reid 1993, 116) notable in *Cycles* is constructed from Davis' uncanny ability to displace notions of time and alterity. *Cycles* is a metanarrative poem built around the central narrative of an African-American woman waiting for her period. Built upon this core is the diegesis of time which is sutured emphatically by an extradiegetic use of the sound of a clock ticking loudly throughout the film. Interjected throughout the multilayered soundtrack, we hear music of Africa, including the singing of Miriam Makeba, Orisha chanting, blues by Clora Bryant, and the Shakeree instrumentation of Darryl Munyungo Jackson. Toni Cade Bambara described this polylogue of sound and imagery as a "Pan-African Esperanto via altars, ve'ves, chants to the Orishas, Haitian music, African music, and a speaking chorus whose individ-

10

ual accents blend US Northern-Southern-Midwestern with African and Caribbean" (128). *Cycles* is drawn in a fittingly spiritual circular pattern. The opening imagery of an altar of an African icon, candles, family photographs, fruit, nuts, and the ritual burning of incense is repeated at the end of the film. Sutured to this cyclical pattern are images of female routine such as body cleansing, vacuuming, mopping, scrubbing, dressing, praying, undressing and cleaning. These repetitive tasks suggest both the routine and the tension of waiting for the menstrual cycle to circle again. As Davis reminds us, "The whole notion of time and having to wait for something to happen, it's very important to the female experience. . . . All women all over the world are waiting for boyfriends, husbands, wives—whatever, waiting for telephones to ring. They're waiting for menstruation to happen" (Filemyr 9). Concomitantly, temporality—time and space and female spiritual reconfigurations of these concepts also occur in Davis' other films, such as *A Powerful Thang* (1991). The end of *Cycles* remaps time across the cinematic construct of the performative film space with the ludic voices of various women testifying to what foods they crave immediately before they menstruate. Davis is at once involved in a poetic trance on the female body and a playful and self-reflexive invitation to her audience to participate in the film's spirituality. Audiences laugh and chime in with their own personal experiences of menstruation. The ability of Zeinabu irene Davis to connect with her audience is indicative of her spiritual belief in connections across time, space, and her invocations of the spirits of her mother, grandmothers, the Orisha and all the ancestors, and to Black filmmakers Kathleen Collins and Hugh Robertson.

In *Cycles*, Davis connects the film body, the filmmaker, and the image of Black woman across time and space, defying the "restricted economy of ethnic enunciation" defined by Isaac Julien and Kobena Mercer (5). Furthermore, the inclusion of multiple narrators in *Cycles* avoids the trap of the double bind of speaking Black subjects wherein a "single film could 'speak for' an entire community of interests [which] reinforces the perceived secondariness of that community" (Julien and Mercer 4). *Cycles* invites the viewer into a diasporic, spiritually-charged space continuum where the Black female body of Stephanie Ingram (who plays Rasheeda Allen) revels in ownership of public and private space as she is continually reinforced by voices that remind her "you're doing O.K. and you're going to get better," and "progress is being made." The disembodied voices become embodied as they reclaim Black female spiritual space. This transgressive use of an extradiegetic voice-over, as Mary Ann Doane writes, "deepens the diegesis, gives it an extent which exceeds that of the image, and thus supports the claim that there is a space in the fictional world which the camera does not register. In its own way, it *accounts for* lost space" (1986, 340). This lost space goes beyond the physical world while at the same time regrounds physical details into spiritual space and time. *Cycles* images remind us that the "corporeal fluidity from images of water. . . . this keeping-alive and life-giving water exists simultaneously as the writer's ink, the mother's milk, the woman's blood and menstruation" (1989, 38) in Trinh T. Minh-ha's words. In *Cycles*, the image that strongly comes to mind is that of a grainy black and white close-up of the wet toes of Rasheeda as she plays with the silver back drain on the tub.

This image of Rasheeda's feet is lush, yet volatile. It is followed by images of Rasheeda immersing herself under the water in the tub and repeatedly turning her body around as if to blur the boundaries between her physical body with the water in the tub, a life-giving spiritual fluid that is further transmogrified by the saxophone off-screen that reaches across the film space in an invitation to join in the Black womanist revelry. Other images in *Cycles* render the importance of African spiritual symbology. The opening credits include a life symbol which repeatedly recurs throughout the film. A young child draws the same symbol in chalk on a sidewalk, literally grinding the sign of the African spirit into the public space. Davis uses memory-edits to flash back to casual moments of Rasheeda with a young Black woman and man. In an amazing stop-frame animation sequence, the group perform a sacred ritual in a tiny space surrounded by modern traffic. All of this transgressive reclamation of space is rendered playfully, as though Davis laughs in the Medusan face of racism and oppression. She refuses to be fragmented by homogeneic inscriptions of Black femaleness. She recognizes that to celebrate the body and spirit, one must be able to understand that "thought is as much a product of the eye, the finger, or the foot as it is of the brain" (Minh-ha 1989, 39). Rasheeda's spirituality and corporeality is unmistakably connected with her smile, her clean sheets, her altar, her copy of Toni Morrison's *Beloved*, her vacuum, her menses, her photographs, her Louis Armstrong and Kassav albums, the voices of Miriam Makeba and the Orisha, and the signifying symbol ground into the sidewalk, and the title of the film: the life-affirming symbol of fluidity, cycles of power.

Zeinabu irene Davis refigures spiritual space beyond the typically accepted codes of mainstream narrative cinema. As Mary Ann Doane explains, in "classical" cinema there are only three spaces: "The space of the diegesis . . . the visible space of the screen as receptor of the image. . . . [and] the acoustical space of the theatre or auditorium" (1986, 339). *Cycles* remaps space in an effort to move beyond these three limited space zones. This is exactly what Davis refers to as the elusive "something going on" (Filemyr 9) that she could not quite put her finger on in describing the film. The remapping of the cinema space is achieved by Davis' notion of a "body as a discontinuous nontotalizable series of processes [cleaning, dancing, chanting, menstruating], organs, flows, energies, corporeal substances [the bloodstained sheet] and incorporeal events, speeds and durations [including the use of pixillation and other image manipulation techniques, all of which] may be of great value to feminists attempting to reconceive bodies outside the binary oppositions imposed on the body by the mind/body, nature/culture, subject/object and interior/exterior oppositions" (Grosz 164). Grosz reads this notion of the body as the *difference* described by Deleuze and Guattari, the transgressive "alternative notions of corporeality and materiality [that] propose quite different, active, affirmative conceptions of desire" (Grosz 165). The space(s) remapped in *Cycles* are somatic, of the body, endlessly spiritual and cyclical, and endlessly transgressive. Furthermore, the film acts upon us, becomes a body, becomes an active gaze that works on us in a widening of the scopic gaze to a fourth look termed "the look back" (Dixon 7) with a hyperreal ability to transform and recreate the viewer's sense of space and time. It is no surprise then that Zeinabu irene Davis locates her film work within a developing African-American aesthetic not unlike that of blues or jazz. The dizzying poetic fervor and flavor of *Cycles* is in some ways comparable with the metronomic contrapuntal space- time movement in the music of Charlie Parker or John Coltrane. The oppositional cinema of Zeinabu irene Davis is inseparable from the body of Davis herself as "oppositional spectator" (hooks 1993, 300) and as one of the many "Black female critical thinkers concerned with creating space for the construction of radical Black female subjectivity" (hooks 1993, 300). As bell hooks writes, African-American women filmmakers of the diaspora "do more than resist. We create alternative texts" (1993, 300).

Zeinabu irene Davis consistently takes risks in her cinema, both in narrative technique and content. Hers is a cinema of and by the Black spirit and female corporeal time/space. The menstrual blood mark of *Cycles* is only one transgression that is part of a continual removal of the veil over femininity and blackness. In *A Powerful Thang* (1991) Davis again discusses and displays bodily functions, sexual toys, and sexual protection that are rarely seen in either classical mainstream (white) narratives or even experimental (white) filmmaking practices. In *A Powerful Thang*, women exchange vibrators, condoms, dental dams, and aphrodisiac teas. In one scene, a lesbian African dance master offers the central heroine, Yasmine, a dental dam, and a vibrator is exchanged. Yasmine's father gives her a bag full of condoms on the eve of her big date. It is one of many "risks" that Davis takes as a filmmaker, but she does it with such panache and grace that we revel in the pleasure of these honest (and responsible) images and of the lyrics of the title song (written and sung by Hattie Gossett), which insists that we use condoms and "dental dams, dental dams, yes dental dams."

Like *Cycles*, *A Powerful Thang* partakes in an oppositional gaze and embraces spirituality across Pan African diasporic time/space configurations. *A Powerful Thang*, however, speaks to the issue of the burden of representation of the African-American woman filmmaker herself. The text of the film becomes inseparable from the body of the *auteur*, herself aware of the importance of the racial economy of representation. As a filmmaking teacher and critic, Zeinabu irene Davis feels that "it is important to be a woman and to be a Black person and to teach the production aspects of filmmaking because I'm not supposed to know how to do it" (Filemyr 8). *A Powerful Thang* self-reflexively comments on the burden of representation and teaching by introducing a central heroine, Yasmine, who is juggling the roles of academic writer, mother, and African-American professor, and is reclaiming her sexuality, after a period of celibacy. In a very funny, yet uncannily unconventional opening scene, Yasmine stares at her computer as she writes an article. In a voice-over she says, "Why is it deadlines for articles always come at the same time I have something better on my mind, like Craig. I'd rather be thinking about tonight than writing this article on Black women's self-image. . . . *They do connect*: Body-image, dating, motherhood, tonight." This skillfully rendered moment signifies the filmmaker on a number of metanarrative levels. Just as Zeinabu irene Davis feels responsible as teacher-filmmaker-mother-lover, so does her central heroine writer Yasmine. Just when the viewer is registering this multileveled signifier, the camera pulls back from a medium shot of Yasmine at the computer to a shot of her son at a typewriter, clearly looking to her as a role model and adding one more facet to her responsibilities. Yasmine has put sex on the back burner for two years, we learn, and she is torn between all of her responsibilities and her newfound desire. The Black womanist burden of representation is the central dialogic crisis in Yasmine, as it is in the film.

As Kobena Mercer argues, the burden of representation is ever present, "whether one is making a film, writing a book, organizing a conference or curating an exhibition, this 'sense of urgency' arises because the cultural reproduction of a certain racism structurally depends on the regulation of Black visibility in the public sphere" (235). *A Powerful Thang* engages in a suture of signifiers that at once responds to, and dialogically recounts the complexity of the burden of representation(s). The suture of displayed opening and closing images include an African statue, a computer, a Black history month poster, an animated (eroticized) bed, a photograph of Martin Luther King, Jr., and an indelible image of the dreadlocked Black heroine, Yasmine, about to use a vibrator to masturbate in an unprecedented reclamation of Black womanist pleasure and the burden of her responsibilities. Davis' use of suture is defined by Kaja Silverman wherein:

> Suture can be understood as a process whereby the inadequacy of the subject's position is exposed in order to facilitate (i.e. create the desire for) new insertions into a cultural discourse. . . . This sleight-of-hand involves attributing to a character within the fiction qualities which in fact belong to the machinery of enunciation. (234)

The machinery of enunciation here is the camera/eye/body of the filmmaker who self- reflexively interrupts the film at one point (during a love-making scene) and allows her assistant director into the frame, where he interrupts Yasmine and her lover, Craig, and says: "Yo! I know this is an independent film. Now Zeinabu doesn't have the money for all these takes. You think you could get it right, y'all?" Davis playfully injects her own body into the text and encourages the viewer to read her as another suture to the text, just in case she missed the many autobiographical connections with the main character. As a filmmaker, Davis is obviously comfortable playing with the concept of the fourth wall, and with the "look back" of the camera/enunciator. Within this context of self-reflexive representation, the voice-over narrator's phrase, "*They do connect*: Body-image, dating, motherhood, tonight," takes on an extra-diegetic quality. As the viewer tries to see how they connect, specifically "this evening," not just the evening in the narrative, but "this" evening that we are viewing this film, we feel a sense of film magic and film viewing pleasure in identification across the fourth wall.

A Powerful Thang excels at the (re)representation of Black femaleness, and Black maleness, equally; both are ground in the image of the body and the rendering of pleasure contrasted with the pain of waiting and misunderstanding. The film unfolds in an almost ethnographic approach to the narrative of a love story which unravels within the extraordinary yet ordinary culture of "Afro-Ohio" (as the film title reads). The film is a poem that includes a mixture of

animation and live action sequences. The main character's need for sexual gra-
tification is placed in contrast with the male character's need to slow down the
relationship and make sure that it is based on love and friendship.

Craig is Yasmine's romantic interest. He plays the tenor sax and also teaches
young Black children music. His horn is a signifier not just of Black masculinity, but also of a much deeper dialogic significance. It comes to life through
pixillated animation. It connects Craig's body to a long tradition of African
musical culture. It is sutured indelibly to the poetry on the soundtrack of Alice
Dunbar Nelson, Paul Laurence Dunbar, and Rita Dove. Craig himself defies
African-American male stereotypical configurations, especially, but not exclusively, with regard to sexuality. Davis surprises us by rendering Craig as sexually sensitive and cautious. He wants to take it slow, but he is pressured by his
friends at the barbershop, by his mother who teases him and makes him aphrodisiac tea, and finally by Yasmine herself, who expects to be seduced on their
first date. Davis explodes the myth of Black male sexual superiority, insa-
tiability, or irresponsibility in one fell swoop. This demythologization of the
Black male body is a direct answer to the burden of representation of Black
male sexuality, one that is informed by a pervasive myth described at length
by Kobena Mercer:

> The notion that Black men have a stronger capacity for sexual enjoyment or
> simply that Black men "do it" more and better . . . [these] images of the threat-
> ening, marauding "buck" tell us more about the "repressed" fears and fantasies
> of European civilization than they do about Black people's experience of sex-
> ual intimacy. (149)

This is not to say that Davis in any way desexualizes or defetishizes the Black
male body. On the contrary, she actively engages in an oppositional gaze that
seeks to objectify through subjectivity, through the guise of Black female spectatorship. The images of Craig's body are sometimes very eroticized and sometimes deeroticized, in a display of playful dialogic female gazing.

The first time we see Craig, he is wearing nothing but shorts as he plays his
horn alone in his bedroom. Davis uses a montage of images of Craig's body,
including close-ups of his thighs, shoulders, and buttocks. Obviously, these
shots are from the erotically charged subjective point of view of Yasmine. Later
in the film, Craig is shown buying and eating an inordinate amount of soul
food at the soul food kitchen and in his mother's kitchen. In the film, we learn
that Craig feels a pressure to conform to a socially produced body image, as a
Black man. Craig resists the burden of representation that is thrust upon Black

men, even within Black male culture. He only feels self-defined when he is alone; driving around listening to disco or playing his saxophone in the corn-fields of Ohio. He confronts his feelings about his body image when he is in the classroom teaching, where, significantly, in a voice-off we hear him asking, "Is she willing to take me as I am?" Clearly Zeinabu Davis is working to break down stereotypes of both African-American men and women.

The (re)construction of the Black body across space/time configurations in *A Powerful Thang* is very much like that worked out in Davis' earlier short Black and white film, *Cycles*. The time that Yasmine spends at home getting ready for her big date is truncated, ellipsed, and formally reconstructed in much the same manner as the time Rasheeda spends waiting for her period in *Cycles*. Again, to quote Yasmine in *A Powerful Thang*, "*They do connect*: Body-image, dating, motherhood, tonight." That Davis effectively sutures a study of female body-image across the questions of sexual representation and body ownership within what often appears to be a traditional narrative film, but which is actually more of a hybridized experimental narrative film, is a testa-ment to her ability to create a new visual language that is reflective of African and African-American female experience.

Yasmine, like Craig, is at once spiritual, sensual and intellectually vibrant. Most of the film takes place, we discover, in a flashback from the opening scene of Yasmine at her computer working on her manuscript and preparing for a date. Davis carefully enunciates the details of Yasmine's evening. We see her preparing an altar, lighting candles, washing her dreadlocks, she gets impatient waiting for Craig to call, she applies some perfume, she gets a call from her editor, she bathes, and again like Rasheeda (in *Cycles*), she *waits*. Yasmine exists in a dream state of waiting and anxiety, combined with moments of pleasure and spiritual self-affirmation. As she applies make-up, we hear her inner voice:

> Putting on make-up and writing this article about Black women's self-image . . . When I put on khoal I feel connected to my desert sisters whose self-pro-tection enhances their beauty. Black women are truly like dense water baskets: Practical, beautiful, artistic, and adaptable.

Yasmine's internally persuasive spiritual voice-over celebrates Black dias-poric female traditions and, as in *Cycles* "accounts for lost space" (Doane 1986, 340). The use of multiple voice-overs and African and Caribbean thumb piano (by Nuiuda fina File Aeena), combined with the sounds of Rufus' "Tell Me Somethin' Good," reclaim diasporic time and space. The voice-overs and music are "first and foremost in the service of the film's construction of space . . . "

(Doane 1986, 340). This diasporic space is neither essentialist nor heterocentric. Davis includes central lesbian characters whom we meet at an African dance class. These women help Yasmine to explore her rich heritage and at the same time encourage her to explore lesbian sexuality. *A Powerful Thang* encourages the viewer to rethink sexuality. It is uncompromisingly meant to teach safe sex, yet at the same time it is an embrace of African-American male and female sexuality of all types.

As Gloria Gibson writes on *A Powerful Thang*, "the film ingeniously pits desire for sexual intimacy against the need for love. [It is] a catalyst for in-depth discussions of intimate relationships" (Women Make Movies 54). Both *Cycles* and *A Powerful Thang* are political films with a sense of humor and pleasure. One of the funniest uses of humor in Black cinema is in *A Powerful Thang* in several pixillated animations of Yasmine's bed. As Zeinabu irene Davis told Ann Filemyr:

> For Yasmine the magic is her bed. The scene where I pixillate—that's a long, tedious process of moving an object and shooting one frame, then moving it again—her bed, which is a futon, changes from a couch to a bed as if to say, "Alright! I'm ready! At last I'm gonna get some use. . . . I mean the bed is ready!" (9)

It is essential to be able to bring a sense of humor to narratives of single Black women and men. Zeinabu irene Davis has had to keep her sense of humor alive as an independent Black woman filmmaker. Her sense of humor is quite apparent in interviews and in the few phone calls that we have shared. Davis decided to become a filmmaker when she was visiting Kenya and Nairobi and she recognized the politics inherent in the ethnographic films being made by German and Belgian documentary film crews in Africa. She calls it the "Mutual of Omaha presents the Wild Kingdom Kind of Thing" (Filemyr 7). She lost her sense of humor when she noticed that white European ethnographers tended to document the Masai people almost exclusively, because they were deemed more "exotic" (thus more easily objectified) than many other African groups. Initially, Davis planned to work on a film with Kenyan author Ngugi wa Thiong'o. However, their plans were suspended when Thiong'o was made a political prisoner. Davis was inspired by Black women filmmakers such as Kathleen Collins, Michelle Parkerson, Alile Sharon Larkin, Ayoka Chenzira and also the early African-American woman filmmaker Eloice Gist, who made spiritual films in the first part of the this century. Davis sees herself as part of a larger tradition of African-American filmmakers going back to the John-

son Brothers, Oscar Micheaux, Zora Neale Hurston (who made some early ethnographic films) and taking off more recently with the films of Julie Dash,
Camille Billops, Daresha Kyi, O. Funmilayo Makarah and many other filmmakers of the African diaspora. Davis has written, produced and directed eight
films and she's had screenings at the Whitney and many film festivals. Davis is
a professor of film and audio production at Northwestern University in Illinois.
She is very outspoken on the need to bring the cinematic apparatus to African-
Americans. She is angered by privileged film academics who often mystify the
production side of film and video. "They are intentionally closing the channels
of expression and communication," she told Ann Filemyr (8). In a phone conversation, Davis and I discussed the problems African-American women face
in mainstream Hollywood production and distribution. She explained that the
probable reason that African- American women directors such as Leslie Harris
(*Just Another Girl on the IRT*) and Darnell Martin (*I Like It Like That*) were not
offered huge multifilm package deals after their success is that Hollywood executives do not think that Black women are a viable commercial audience (Foster interview).

Davis is unstintingly supportive of both mainstream and independent
Black directors and would-be directors. At the same time, she argues that independent filmmaking is getting harder to support, especially with the col-
lapse of funding sources such as the National Endowments of the Arts and
Humanities. Even with governmental fiscal support, independent filmmakers
must be able to be "part hustler, part collaborator, part compromiser, part
real persistence" (Filemyr 8). Nevertheless, Davis continues to maintain her
filmmaking career. Her most recent work is a half-hour film entitled *Mother
of the River*, which was produced for I.T.V.S. The film "concerns a young slave
girl who is full of magic," Davis told me (Foster interview). *Mother of the River*
is geared toward the female adolescent audience ignored by mainstream
cinema.

One of the most important ways in which Black women filmmakers can
convey a positive message to African-American girls is to provide role models
of young female heroines, for as Gloria Gibson writes, "Black women independent filmmakers hope that all audiences will understand how the characters' maturation and subsequent empowerment on the screen can function to
strengthen their own personal knowledge and consciousness" (367).

Zeinabu irene Davis' *Mother of the River* (1995) is the narrative of a young
slave girl, Dofimae (played by Adrienne Coleman), who provides a role model
of independence, spirituality, determination, loyalty, and community-minded-

ness that is, unfortunately, a rarity among television movies or feature films. As Zeinabu irene Davis told me, she made the film about a slave girl's experiences because she found, as a teacher, that:

> most people know very little about slavery and even less about women's experiences as slaves. Many people would rather forget slavery. I think it is important that we remember. There have been many films on slavery, but not too many are from the viewpoint of a young girl. (Foster interview)

Mother of the River is based on the legend of a relationship between a young girl and an ostracized old woman. The story recurs throughout Africa and the African diaspora. The story tends to stress community values such as honor, respect, humility, love and self-respect. The screenplay for the film was written by Marc Arthur Chery, Davis' Haitian-born husband (who also co-wrote *A Powerful Thang* and numerous other screenplays). Chery chose to set the African legend on a Southern plantation in the ante-bellum South of the 1850s. The film gracefully evokes African spirituality as it co-existed with Christian beliefs of the period. Dofimae finds a spiritual guide in the embodiment of Mother of the River (played by Joy Vandervort). Dofimae provides young African-American girls with a role model who, as Barbara Christian comments:

> must return to her source, must remember the ancient wisdom of African culture—that the body and the spirit are one, that harmony cannot be achieved unless there is a reciprocal relationship between the individual and the community—if she is to define herself as a Black woman. (243)

Mother of the River is an African-American *bildungsroman* specifically made for young African-American women, eager for reflections of their own image. Dofimae travels on a spiritual journey, and becomes an action heroine who saves Mother of the River, providing an invaluable, yet rarely seen, role model, a young Black action heroine. Davis and Chery endow the character Dofimae with brilliance and super-heroine abilities. As the film unravels, we meet Dofimae, the riddle teller, a bright young woman who is eager to learn the art of storytelling from her father. Again the film provides a role-model for African-American girls that is unusual, that of the signifying, speaking, young Black female presence. Dofimae transgresses the boundaries of the archetypal silenced young slave girl, as sadly typified in both filmic and literary depictions of slavery. More than simply being present, Dofimae eats up the screen with her exuberance and story-telling ability. Another transgression is her relationship with a young white girl, who is drawn to Dofimae's wit. The White mistress (the girl's mother) puts an end to their relationship; however, the film teaches both young Black and White audiences that racism cannot separate true friends.

One day Dofimae meets Mother of the River, who has been injured by a bullet wound in an act of heroism as part of the underground railroad. Mother of the River teaches Dofimae about Pan African spirituality. She gives Dofimae magical eggs and shows her how she can fly from the South to the North, aiding slaves in their quest for freedom. When Dofimae starts asking questions about "the North," the white plantation owners become suspicious and the overseers begin to whip Dofimae. Mother of the River, however, disrupts the beating by flying across the sky, and magically putting an end to the harrowing scene. A chase ensues, and the overseers corner Mother of the River. Dofimae uses the magical eggs to save Mother of the River. She stops the bullets from their guns in mid-flight by firing the magic eggs with a slingshot. At the end of the film, Mother of the River promises to return to help Dofimae and her family to freedom.

Zeinabu irene Davis' interest in African folklore and Pan African spirituality is apparent in all of her films. She developed her knowledge of the area while studying in Kenya as an undergraduate. The importance of reclaiming traditions and lost knowledge is of utmost importance to African-Americans because, as Davis told Ted Shen, "Even under colonialism, Africans lived on their own land. Here we suffer from racial discrimination and feel displaced. We still don't know where we came from. We must create our own traditions" (6).

For the screenplay of *Mother of the River*, Davis and her husband, Marc Chery, chose a Haitian tale and renarrated it among the landscape of a South Carolina plantation. The eggs that Dofimae is given by Mother of the River signify fertility and potency in African culture. *Mother of the River* draws upon this tradition, which developed in the South as the ritual of using eggs to protect the self or to put hexes on enemies. The Haitian tale, in turn, is drawn from a Nigerian tale in which two girls, one good and one bad, experience a coming of age. *Mother of the River* is a brilliant retelling of a traditional folk tale that celebrates the power of the speaking girl child. Like African-American women's fiction and poetry, Davis' films signify and hold the power to heal through the art of storytelling. The words of these women bespeak and enact alterity and subjectivity from a Black woman's perspective. As Charlotte Watson Sherman writes in *Sisterfire*, they "encompass the Black female experience from a womanist perspective. They speak to the lives of contemporary Black women [and children], raise our voices, and help make us visible" (xviii).

The strength of the African-American community lies in the healing abilities of life affirming tale-telling and image-making. Zeinabu irene Davis celebrates the opportunity to tell stories about Black people that haven't been told before, or that have been lost in cultural erasure. Her next film, *Compensation*, is told from the perspective of a hearing-impaired African-American woman. Davis has been working to reclaim lost spiritual legacies, and to change Black women's images since her very first films, *Recreating Black Women's Media Images* (1987) and *Crocodile Conspiracy* (1986). *Crocodile Conspiracy* focuses on the spiritual journey of an African-American schoolteacher who returns to her parents' homeland, Cuba, despite political and familial interference. Perhaps one of the reasons Davis herself is able to overcome all types of interference and obstacles is that her name "Zeinabu" means "spirited sparrow" in Swahili, conjuring images of flight and independence. Davis took the name when she was in Nairobi and her friend, the writer Ngugi wa Thiong'o, found "Irene" too difficult to pronounce. Soon she was dubbed Zeinabu, the sparrow, and she took the name and relegated irene to her middle name, minus the capital. Zeinabu irene Davis' self-naming is another form of moving out of the objectified position of African-American woman into the active, subjective identity.

Zeinabu irene Davis is quick to recognize the tradition of African-American women directors that has been all but obliterated in mainstream film history and criticism. As she told Ted Shen, she sees herself carrying the torch of women directors such as the evangelist Eloice Gist, "whose message about evils of sins, in my opinion are more sophisticated than Oscar Micheaux's" (6). Davis also cites the influences of women such as Zora Neale Hurston, who made ethnographic films in addition to her more famous literary achievements. Among her other influences, Davis mentions Camille Billops, Jackie Shearer, Daresha Kyi, Ellen Sumter, Dawn Suggs, and of course, Julie Dash, and in particular, Michelle Parkerson, because of her courage as a Black lesbian artist who was one of the first to document African-American women artists in films such as *But Then, She's Betty Carter* (1980), *Sweet Honey in the Rock* (1983), and *Stormé: The Lady of the Jewel Box* (1987).

Perhaps most strenuously, however, Davis cites the work of Ayoka Chenzira as an influence and an independent filmmaking sister. Chenzira, like Davis, draws upon Pan African spirituality in her work and remakes images of African-American people against the grain of Hollywood representation. *Zajota and the Boogie Spirit* (1989), and *Secret Sounds Screaming* (1986) are videos by Chenzira that testify to the sexual abuse of children. *Syvilla, They Dance to Her Drum* documents a generation of African-American dance and the contribution of choreographer Syvilla Fort. *The Lure and the Lore* (1988) documents the performance artist Thomas Pinnock, who draws upon traditional lore of his native Jamaican heritage to create his choreography.

Chenzira's most famous film is probably *Hair Piece* (1985). *Hair Piece* is an animated film that deals with African-American women's hairstyles, is in some ways comparable with the auto-ethnographic films of Zeinabu irene Davis. Both filmmakers use animation, humor, and bodily self-inscription to reclaim subjectivity for Black women. *Hair Piece*, like *Cycles* and *A Powerful Thang*, adopts an oppositional gaze. As Ayoka Chenzira told Afua Kafi-Akua, she made the film to rethink the images and self-images of African-American culture. "One of the things I talk about in *Hair Piece* is that I think how you present yourself says a lot about who you think you are and in my mind most of us are really presenting ourselves as though we think we are of an inferior and deficient model" (71).

Hair Piece is not a monologic criticism of African-American hair culture, instead it is a dialogic discourse that embraces diasporic practices of Black stylization, while at the same time it engages in a ludic playful study of Black female hair culture. This dialogic response is not surprising in light of the fact that Black hairstyling is immersed in a cultural admixture of a history of oppressive colonialist marking of the body and a more recent celebration of self-stylization. In a lengthy discussion of the semiotics and politics of hair, Kobena Mercer explains that inscription and expression are both important modes of Black stylization:

> The patterns and practices of aesthetic stylization developed by Black cultures in the West may be seen as modalities of cultural struggle inscribed in critical engagement with the dominant white culture and at the same time expressive of a neo-African approach to the pleasures of beauty at the level of everyday life. (114)

The cultural politics of Black hair stylization also come into play in the films of Julie Dash and Zeinabu irene Davis. African-American women directors, through their texts on film and their critical texts, are posing the question "Whose cinema is this?" and "Whose body is this?" It is important to recognize that these filmmakers are engaged in a battle of the ethics of ethnographic representation. It is only when "films are impressed and, indeed, possessed by their subjects: when they become bound into a relationship with the subject as part of a larger set of meanings" (MacDougall 1994a, 33) that we can fully consider the question "Whose story is this?"

NGOZI ONWURAH
"A different concept and agenda"

BLACK DIASPORIC CORPOREALITY—the body—is the mise-en-scène of Black British filmmaker Ngozi Onwurah. Onwurah consistently navigates and challenges the limits of narrative and ethnographic cinema by insisting that the body is the central landscape of an anti-imperialist cinematic discourse. Onwurah's films address the Western ethnographic texts that objectify non-European "subjects" as "the Other" in one of the most specious and persistent acts of colonial domination. However, as Jennifer Barker persuasively argues:

> The authority of the Western ethnographic text, and that of narrative theories which claim the cohesive, all-encompassing authority of the implied author and the narrational system as whole, is not so easily asserted. These narrative and theoretical systems fail to account for one inescapable and powerful presence: the body. (66)

Onwurah magnifies the disruptive force of the body in her films and in the process opens up an intertextural anti-colonialist cinema practice. Recognizing the need for an autobiographical approach to ethnography, Onwurah creates an "auto-ethnography," such as that described by Bill Nichols, one that opens up "dialogue, debate, and fundamental reconceptualization" (64). Onwurah's cinema stands in direct contrast to traditional ethnographic (and I would add, narrative) cinema that suppresses knowledge and contains bodies. As Bill Nichols comments, the "anthropologist filmmaker usually disappears behind the optical vantage point where camera and filmmaker preside . . . transforming first-hand, personal experience into third person disembodied knowledge" (68). The disembodied voice of authority is disrupted most radically in Onwurah's *And Still I Rise* (1993) when the "subject," an African woman, directly addresses and criticizes the disembodied voice of authority.

And Still I Rise, inspired by a poem by Maya Angelou, is an examination of ethnographic films, particularly African and other Black women's images in colonialist documentary practice. The film opens with a parody of the typical colonial ethnographic paradigm, an African woman viewed as the subject while a disembodied white male voice describes (and contains) her:

> She walked with measured steps, treading the earth proudly with a jingle and flash of barbarous ornaments. She carried her head high with a crimson spot on her tawny cheek, innumerable glass beads on her neck. Bizarre things. Charms. Gifts of witchmen glittered and trembled at every step. She was *savage* and *superb*. Wild-eyed and magnificent.

Suddenly the subject speaks, moving from object status to subjective identity. At once speaking to the viewer and also the disembodied voice-over, she mocks: "*Sultry. Savage. Dirty. Hard. Exotic.* Many people have trouble seeing Black women as they are because of an eagerness to impose an identity on us." Her disembodied knowledge becomes embodied, and the important work of testifying and breaking down filmic boundaries begins. The central woman narrator is joined by the voices of a multitude of narrators who, like early African-American women writers, for example, use their status as speaking subject insider informant. As Frances Smith Foster writes, women narrators are actively "testifying to the fact of their existence and insisting that others acknowledge their existence and their testimonies . . . consciously creating new criteria against which the testimonies of others might be judged" (2).

Among the testifying auto-ethnographers in *And Still I Rise*, Onwurah includes a multivoiced range of Black women who speak the body through the history of colonial domination. Singer/songwriter Caron Wheeler explains that her body, her sexuality, has been inscribed in a history of pain and rape, both in her life and in her ancestors' lives. The body of an African slave woman, naked and bound, illustrated in an eighteenth century colonial text is interspliced in the film and underscored with a loud crack of a whip and the cry of a horse. As the film continues to unfold, another narrator, Dr. Christopher Davis, a social anthropologist, explains the psychology and economic imperatives behind the history of the ownership of Black female bodies. When Europeans colonized West Africa in the seventeenth century they saw only nakedness and assumed that there were no codes of kinship—only "barbarity." The sexuality of African women (and men) was coded as something that needed to be contained and "civilized." The economics of slavery needed to be supported by theories to "justify" the mistreatment and torture of the Black body and African people. As Stella Dadzie says in the film, "You had a whole range of theories about Black people, Black sexuality, Black social behavior, which were designed to justify the basic idea that Europeans *had the right* to go in and

rape African land and African people and steal their human material and re-
sources."

And Still I Rise continues with the documentation of the history of the rape
and torture of African women's bodies and in doing so directly confronts painful imagery, as does Jean Rouch, a French ethnographic filmmaker who was
lambasted for his ability to "document the unthinkable" (Stoller 85) and whose
films were dubbed "the cinema of cruelty," in an effort to dismiss his cinema,
which was anticolonialist, antiracist, and antiimperialist. Onwurah also documents the unthinkable, that which seeks to testify to the pain inscribed in
Black women, particularly with regard to sexuality. *And Still I Rise* documents
what many Europeans, and perhaps even some Africans and African-Americans, would rather not address. The rape of African women became institutionalized by slavery, the filmmaker explains; in many cases slaveowners used
rape as a tool of submission, "like breaking in a horse," and the myth that
women "enjoyed it" was perpetuated in order to further subjugate Black women
and Black sexuality. Some critics may have problems with Onwurah's unflinching approach, her documentation of the unthinkable, but as Manthia Diawara
writes in his essay "Black American Cinema: The New Realism," the cultural
work of Black independent cinema must produce more than simplistic "positive images" that can "serve the function of plotting Black people in white
space and white power" (1993, 12). Ngozi Onwurah maps ethnographies of
Black corporeal space and marks out territories of anger and unflinching criticism of colonialist discourse. For example, historian Barbara Bush, interviewed
within *And Still I Rise*, reminds us that Victorian Europeans engaged in the
invention of supposedly "scientific evidence" that Africans had smaller brains
and larger sexual organs. Onwurah reenacts this colonialist scene with the visual representation of Africans being "measured" and objectified. These practices have reappeared in writings such as *The Bell Curve* and in more recent
postcolonial efforts to rationalize institutional racism and further the motives
of institutionalized racism.

And Still I Rise moves to counter such practices and also to remake ethnographic cinema practice. The use of multiple narrators, multiple subjects, and
multiple subjectivities moves disembodied knowledge into the body of the
film itself and ultimately into the viewer. *And Still I Rise* is itself a viewer, looking back at the first world viewer, indeed, looking back at European history
as an object of inquiry. Onwurah's films exemplify the "nomadic" cinema described by Teshome Gabriel:

[one that] brings an unprecedented and unexpected jolt to cinematic reality by smashing down boundaries—between documentary, ethnographic, travelogue, experimental and narrative fiction. . . . It brings the unknown to recognition, the unrepresentable to representation. (1988, 73)

And Still I Rise ends with a call for Black women to own their own sexualities and multiple identities. The film revels in "a nomadic type of feminist theory," as described by Rosi Braidotti, one "where our discontinuities, transformations, shifts of levels and locations can be accounted for . . . " (172). A nomadic, multivoiced, auto-ethnographical approach is clearly being worked out in Onwurah's earliest film, *Coffee Colored Children* (1988), the performative autodocumentary.

Coffee Colored Children blurs the boundaries between autobiographical cinema, experimental cinema, and ethnographic cinema. It is a poetic, black and white, short film, in which the violence, pain, and degradation of children of mixed parentage is fully articulated. This auto-ethnographical film addresses the unspeakable, almost immediately at the beginning of the film. A young white skinhead smears excrement on the front door of the central narrator's childhood home. The film alludes to documentary practice by showing framed pictures of the "subjects," the children who undergo racial harassment, self-hatred, and the ghastly memories of the internalized effects of racism. The central voice-over is embodied in the visuals of a young girl who hated her own reflection and who felt completely isolated and alienated. "We were so strange. The only Black children in the area. The first. We had no father and a white mother." The narrator, like Ngozi Onwurah, was born in Nigeria to a white British mother and a Nigerian father. When Nigeria was undergoing civil war, her mother and her two children were sent to England. The pain and humiliation that both children suffered is recorded, reenacted, and graphically exorcised by a final sequence of burning all of the symbolic referents of pain in a scene of enduring power and significance. Ngozi Onwurah (and the narrator of *Coffee Colored Children*) throw off the shackles of the burden of representation of what has been termed "the tragic mulatto." As Alile Sharon Larkin notes, "The Tragic Mulatto is the Black who is constantly told she/he is neither Black nor white but a hybrid. Seeking her/his identity becomes the primary preoccupation" (160). *Coffee Colored Children* exposes the lie behind the unquestioned celebration of the so-called melting pot ("melting pot or incinerator," the narrator asks) and testifies on behalf of the "coffee colored children" who were "used at school for tag." Included are extremely disturbing sequences in which the children try literally to scrub off their skin with harsh cleansers. The soundtrack is a melange of the children's voice-overs, children's taunting songs, and the voice-overs of the grown-up adults looking at their own internalized painful images. The brother explains (from the adult point of view) how he could not draw himself in art class with a brown face. The sister admits that she wanted to grow up to be a "white princess," a "wonder woman." Extradiegetic noises of scrubbing are overlaid on the soundtrack. Children's voices sing "Ba ba, Blacksheep and Eeeney Meeney Miney Mo," and the children continue to self-mutilate themselves with peroxide and cleansers. Onwurah refuses to be victimized as the "tragic mulatto," nor does she allow her auto-ethnographical filmic representatives to be unable to move beyond the stereotype of "tragic mulatto." In unflinchingly speaking the pain through multiple voices and in imaging the pain, Onwurah turns pain into agency. *Coffee Colored Children* becomes a weapon of agency against pain and further self-mutilation. As an auto- ethnography, *Coffee Colored Children* acts out real pain and torture. No longer is the pain contained within the boundary of the sufferer's body, because, as Elaine Scarry explains, "What assists the conversion of absolute pain into the fiction of absolute power is an obsessive, self-conscious display of *agency*" (my emphasis, 27).

The excesses of the body and pain are moved into the realm of embodied onto logical experience, having an impact upon both the "subject" and the viewer (who, in a sense, becomes a subject). Images of pain have an effect that is physical and corporeal. As Steven Shaviro reminds us, "Perception is turned back upon the body of the perceiver, so that it affects and alters the body, instead of merely constituting a series of representations, for the spectator to recognize" (50). *Coffee Colored Children*, like all of Onwurah's films, is intensely corporeal. The body is a central metaphor for both colonialist oppression and a vehicle for agency. This preoccupation with the body, visual pain, and visual pleasure rises to a crescendo with the final primal scene of catharsis through the agency of the film medium; however, Onwurah problematizes the issue of the politics of bringing racially mixed children into the world. The voice of the female narrator suddenly and markedly redirects her address, with the statement, "Who am I talking to now? . . . My child." After voicing her love to her child, the narrator vows that "the man I love may be white but the father of my child will be Black." The narrator admits that she can't alter the world or its treatment of "coffee colored" children. *Coffee Colored Children* takes issue with the political machinery of melting pot thinking and describes it as a dangerous lie, a failure, "an incinerator." This is a radical gesture; for the ethnographic film traditionally operates "on the assumption that it can and should alter the world itself or our place within it" (Nichols 63).

The difference between *Coffee Colored Children* and Onwurah's next film, *The Body Beautiful,* is a marked shift of authorship. In *Coffee Colored Children,* Onwurah displaces her autobiographical voice to some extent, while *The Body Beautiful* is not only narrated from the point of view of Ngozi Onwurah herself, but is co-narrated by the filmmaker's mother, Madge Onwurah, who also plays herself in the film. It is impossible to decide whose story the film is: the mother's story of marrying a Nigerian, raising two mixed children, and dealing with breast cancer and a mastectomy, or the daughter's story of growing up in a different image than her white mother, being objectified by a white male gaze as a model, admitting to being unable to see her mother as a sexual being, and finally realizing how to be her mother's daughter. The film is obviously, on one level, an auto-ethnography. It is Onwurah's narrative; her editing, image-making and mise-en-scène. On the other hand, the film certainly belongs to Madge Onwurah as well. Because she appears in the film she becomes a coauthor. *The Body Beautiful* demonstrates the difficulty of answering the question, "whose story?" because it engages in multiple identities. Onwurah problematizes authorship, recognizing that "the question of 'whose story?' has both ontological and moral dimensions" (MacDougall 1994a, 29). These ontological and moral dimensions in turn reflect back on the ethnographic process itself, on filmmaking, and on the politics of representation.

True to form, Onwurah presents images in *The Body Beautiful* that court taboo, reflecting that which is often deemed unrepresentable, painful, unknowable, disruptive, even ugly. The film opens with a painful image of an argument between mother and (then) adolescent daughter. "You titless cow!" the daughter screams, as she accuses her mother of never doing anything in life. The strain in their relationship is at the core of the narrative, and it is visually mapped in the body of the mother in the next scene in which the mother and daughter lie naked together. The camera observes the missing breast and scar of the mother, and the audience is forced into confirming and identifying across the visual apparatus with the unspeakable, the unspoken, the veiled image of a scar of mastectomy that has been rendered an image of greater taboo than almost any other image in the sexual and corporeal economy of body imagery. What is the body beautiful in Western society? Onwurah gazes at this question, through the imagery of the scar, and the scar itself becomes a simu-lacra of all the baggage in Western culture strapped onto women's images of beauty and the measurement of women in the sexual economy of the body.

In a typical evocation of the oppositional critical Black gaze, Onwurah opens up the cinematic representation of women by enunciating that which has been rendered taboo. The scar of the mastectomy stares at the viewer, much in the same manner that the Black filmmaker interrogates the gaze of the Othered Western male gaze, looking back and naming the pain. It is important to note that the scar signifies the memory of the senses of pain and pleasure. As Nadia Seremetakis writes, "The points of the body once awakened are not merely marks on the surface but are an active capacity. Awakening these points as sensate is opening the body to semiosis" (216). The suture of the vicious re-mark on the soundtrack ("You titless cow!") across the representation of the scar demonstrates a remarkable filmic fissure of the sensory memory of pain. Seremetakis writes, "The memory of one sense is stored in another: that of tactility in sound, of hearing in taste, of sight and sound" (216). Onwurah's mining of the memory of the senses, her memory of her senses, both in *Coffee Colored Children* and *The Body Beautiful,* grinds her authorial signature in the frame and the sound in ways that are designed to tap into the stored pain of sensory memory and alter it through the filmmaker's journey. Onwurah's map-ping of the memory of her mother's senses is transgressive, yet understandable within the semiotic economy of the mother-daughter exchange system. This bound energy has as immeasurable amount of capacity for healing, yet it is difficult to render on film because of the audience's tendency to separate their identification amongst bodies of individuals. The mother-daughter economy of the senses is the shared frame of *The Body Beautiful.* The fragmented nar-ratorial style of the film marks a return to the senses, which "can never be a return to realism . . . always mediated by memory and assembled from sensory and experiential fragments, this assemblage will always be an act of imagina-tion—thus opposed to the reductions of realism" (Seremetakis 217).

As the camera pans across the bodies of mother and daughter to reveal the scar of the mastectomy, the voice-over narrates the life of the filmmaker her-self. The film revisits the pain of the mother's preparation for the mastectomy and fight with the cancer inside her. A cold clinical authorial voice-over an-nounces, "It's important for you to realize that you're far from being the first woman to face the prospect of losing a breast. These days we do more mastec-tomies than tonsillectomies." The voice enunciates the painful memory of the medical profession's dismissal of women's rights of ownership over her own body, her own pain, her lack of voice in the medical arena.

The authorial voice shifts back and forth between mother and daughter as their story unfolds. As the daughter embarks upon a career as a model we hear Madge Onwurah: "I watched as she joined the elite breed of women penciled in by men who define the sliding scale of beauty that stops at women like me. I had been muted. The daughter, as filmmaker, retrieves her mother's memories and sees through their lines the pain rendered by the beauty system that separated them yet gave the daughter a great deal of pleasure in the beauty of her own body. In a scene in which the pair go to a bathhouse, the daughter is forced to recognize that she has never understood how others might view her mother. As the mother falls asleep, her towel drops away from her missing breast and all of the women in the shower gaze on with looks of shame and horror. In the next scene, the daughter and mother envision the mother having sex with a young Black man. The forbidden fantasy remakes the sexual economy of racial bodies. The mother voices her fantasy to be "desired for my body and not in spite of it." The daughter voices her fantasy to resexualize her mother's body through imagining/imaging this scene. Intercut with the lovemaking scene, the daughter laughs and puts makeup on her own cleavage as she revels in the pleasure of her own body and the body of her eroticized mother. The scene threatens to objectify the Black male body, yet the filmmaker subverts objectification by intercutting a voice-over of the white male authority (a doctor) describing how a woman should have no problems getting along after a mastectomy. This disembodied voice-over figure, first heard at the beginning of the film, is used deliberately by the filmmaker to displace the eroticized gaze of the viewer. The audience is moved into a distanced, critical stance, where he/she is reminded of the mother's ordeal at the hands of the medical establishment. The pleasurable sexual image is marked by the mother's pain, and sexual objectification of the Black male body becomes problematized. A voice-over of the daughter interrupts the scene, screaming at the man, "touch her you bastard," when his hand comes near the mastectomy scar. There is no question that the filmmaker here claims ownership of the scene (which is co-owned by her mother). The filmmaker and her mother control the gaze, the image, the film.

Madge Onwurah and Ngozi Onwurah move from objectified bodies to subjective identities. In the final image of the film, the women lie naked together embracing. The daughter reflects upon her own struggle for a sense of image:

A child is made in its parents image. But to a world that sees only Black and white, I was made only in the image of my father. Yet my mother has molded me. . . . fought for me, protected me . . . I may not be reflected in her image but my mother is mirrored in my soul. I am my mother's daughter for the rest of my life.

The enunciative power of the filmmaker's naming herself her mother's daughter records the exchange from object to subject in a corporeal exchange system in which "the act of calling and naming is also an act of exchange. . . . The transcription of self onto substance and then into the child's body is inseparable from the transmission of emotions as a fuel for this exchange" (Seremetakis 216). The exchanges of sensory memory and experience across and between mother and daughter render the film as a medium of exchange of bodily senses. Onwurah works in that constantly evolving stage of memory image-making that reworks the boundaries of narrative and ethnographic films. Nevertheless, as James Clifford comments, "the subjectivities produced in these often unequal exchanges—whether of 'natives' or of visiting participant-observers—are constructed domains of truth, serious fictions" (10). The serious fictions produced by *The Body Beautiful* are emphatically multivocal, especially with regard to mother-daughter authorial signatures and authorial intents. However, I agree with Bill Nichols, who claims that films like *The Body Beautiful* do not need to be analyzed so much as experienced (15).

The Body Beautiful and *Coffee Colored Children* are sutured by the image of the veil. In both films the central female protagonist, who is to a large extent the alter ego of the filmmaker herself, spends considerable time playing with (or struggling with) a veil. In the case of *Coffee Colored Children*, the young girl wraps herself in a white wedding veil as she attempts to scrub the blackness off of her skin. In *The Body Beautiful*, the veil recurs most blatantly in the fantasy sex scene, which is shrouded in draped veils, and in numerous scenes in which the central heroine, Ngozi's stand-in, seductively plays with a veil, often in a mirror. Gloria Gibson writes that "the veil or mask is a recurring symbol incorporated in Black film and literature" (371). The veil is dialogized as a signifier of the shroud that silences Black women's sexuality, and yet it can also represent a liberating force, a reclamation of Black female space, the female gaze, the scars of the body, and a new skin of self-ownership. Onwurah's continual ludic play with the image of the veil, especially as an eroticized trope in *The Body Beautiful*, combined with the ritual burning of the white wedding veil in *Coffee Colored Children*, demonstrates the filmmaker's mastery of the veil as a multifaceted representation of the scopic (the visual) and the haptic (the corporeal) knowledge invested in the overloaded signifier of the veil. The veil is at once a shifting signifier that moves between signing captivity (in patriarchal hegemonic discourse) and freedom (as a liberated speaking subject). Veiling and unveiling act to "reappropriate space or to claim anew difference, in defiance of genderless hegemonic standardization" (Minh-ha 1991, 151).

It is deeply significant that Onwurah invokes the mask and masquerade in the trope of the "masked image" in both *Coffee Colored Children* and *The Body Beautiful* because she inverts the traditional European gaze that seeks to encase the body of women, and Black women in particular, in an exotic mask, a clinical shroud of medical discourse, and a fetishized object in fashion discourse. In *Coffee Colored Children*, the filmmaker burns the wedding veil signifying defiance of societal codes that only see skin in binary terms of Black and white. In *The Body Beautiful*, she attacks the clinical gaze of the medical establishment that seeks to deny her mother's pain and mask her removed breast. The unveiling of the mastectomy scar rejects the eyes of medical discourse. In the process, the film reminds us of the patriarchal European configurations of femininity as a reminder of "elements which constantly threaten to infiltrate and contaminate that which is more central, health or masculinity" as Mary Ann Doane explains (1987, 38). Ownership of the body of both the scopic and haptic zones of the body: the skin and embodiedness, corporeality is Onwurah's project.

In a brilliantly executed scene in *The Body Beautiful*, the young model stands before a mirror and removes a veil from her breasts. She tries to imagine what it might be like to not have a breast. "It is pointless," she concludes, "like trying to imagine being blind." This is the final recognition of the mask and masquerade between women. It is an acceptance of difference between mother and daughter, and on a larger scale, a political statement about difference. The real world of racial difference, which is so often denied by overdetermined essentialist feminist proscriptions, is unveiled as a masquerade itself. As Onwurah cannot know the experience of her mother's mastectomy, we as viewers cannot know the experience of growing up in Britain with Black skin and a white mother. We can identify to some extent, but we risk essentialism if we attempt to speak of a unified woman subject as a monologic representative of the feminine. In this manner, Onwurah displaces visual pleasure and identification and demands subjectivity. The mask and the veil appear as "signs of the same need for, and a very similar drive toward, the representation of a subjectivity that, however diverse its sociohistorical configurations and modes of expression, has come into its own as political consciousness," according to Teresa de Lauretis (1986, 17).

The cinema of Ngozi Onwurah threatens to remake subjectivity outside of the shrouding, veiling discourses of film theory that so often focus on the psychoanalytic over the phenomenological, the mind over the body. As Bill Nichols argues, the phenomenological tradition "takes considerable interest in the question of the body and how embodied action—performance—constitutes a sense of self in relation to others. . . . It brings into focus the (largely absent) body of the filmmaker him or herself as the organizing locus of knowledge" (72).

By foregrounding the body, the auto-ethnographic films of Ngozi Onwurah engage in what feminist anthropologist Allison Jablonko terms "haptic learning, learning through bodily identification" (182). Moving across the boundaries of visual pleasure, both scopic and haptic, Onwurah carves out a space for the skin, the body, the uncontained and uncontainable vessel of subjectivity. The body as haptic and scopic is irreducible and yet embodied. As Jennifer Barker explains, "the body as excess presents such a problem for current theories . . . that posit narration as cohesive, unambiguous containment of different and contradicting voices within the text" (68).

Ngozi Onwurah's films are similar to those of Trinh T. Minh-ha in that they both address assumptions behind narrative theory and ethnographic theory, as well as the larger issues around the representation of difference. It is imperative to recognize that these works, as Bill Nichols concludes:

> draw much of their inspiration from elsewhere, from other traditions, other forms, other perspectives and emphases . . . they invite "us" to reflect on the current state of, and discourse about, ethnographic [and narrative] film tradition that have sought to represent others when, "we" [white Europeans] have been told they could not represent themselves. (91)

Self-representation owns both filmic space, haptic space, and cultural space in *Monday's Girls* (1993) and *The Desired Number* (1994), Onwurah's more straightforward ethnographic film. In *Monday's Girls*, Onwurah documents two young Nigerian women's different experiences of the traditional rite of passage of the ceremony in which young virgins, iriabo, spend five weeks in "fattening rooms" and emerge to be celebrated and confirmed as women of their community. Onwurah cautiously avoids the traditional ethnographic objectification and silencing of African subjects by strategically choosing to allow the self-representation of the speaking women, Florence, who is honored to take part in the ceremony, and Asikiye, who has been Westernized by living in an urban environment and who finds the ceremony intolerable. In choosing to juxtapose Asikiye and Florence, Onwurah avoids the typical Western-centered binaristic judgmental approach that would seek to represent the African ceremony as sexist and "savage." *Monday's Girls* inverts the cultural paradigm within which most ethnographic films operate, the realm of imperialist nostalgia and what has been called "the white man's burden," or as Renato Rosaldo defines it:

> a peculiar sense of mission, "the white man's burden,"—where civilized nations stand duty-bound to uplift so-called savage ones . . . static savage societies become a stable reference point for defining the felicitous progress of civilized identity. (1993a, 70)

Monday's Girls refutes the example of the "savage" reference point, one that constructs easily read "Third World subjects for first world consumption" (Arora 293). Instead, Onwurah documents the plurality of tradition, modernity, and the speaking subjectivities of Florence and Asikiye. Like *The Body Beautiful, Monday's Girls* moves across boundaries of scopic and haptic knowledge, letting women bespeak the pleasure and pain of the rituals. The scenes of the young girls being celebrated and worshipped, through body-painting, feeding, and dancing, are indelibly corporeal. When the girls wear large copper coils on their legs and learn the traditional dances they talk about their feelings and relate the joy of the experience, as well as their boredom and discomfort. Florence emerges from the ritual with palpable pride, exuberance, and a sense of herself as "a real woman now," a woman of community, while Asikiye is unable to bare her naked breasts and is thus disqualified from the proceedings because of her Westernization.

Monday's Girls forces the question of conflicting interpretations of cultural ideologies and culturally defined senses of space. The iriabo women clearly own the spaces of the fattening rooms, therefore they own space in a way not usually represented by a Western gaze. This rendering space ownership defies Western feminism's insistence that all women have been trapped in a captive domestic space that oppresses them. As cultural anthropologist Henrietta L. Moore confirms "the plurality of culture and the existence of alternative interpretations and values are not usually emphasized in the symbolic analysis of space, or indeed in the symbolic analysis of any form of cultural representation" (74).

Space is not read through a colonialized gaze in *Monday's Girls*, nor is the female body. Women of the African village have alternative models of the world and the gendered organization of space. Their traditional world view is encroached upon by the actions of Asikiye. Asikiye brings with her the acquired sense of shame and privacy she feels about her body as she reads through her Westernized cultural self-representation. She has shamed her family because she was unable to bare her naked breasts in front of the entire village. The conflict between African models and Western models of knowledge are highlighted in the case of family planning issues in *The Desired Number* (1994); (also known as *A Question of Numbers*).

The Desired Number refers to the number of children that is traditionally hoped for in the families of the Iwollo village in Nigeria where women usually have at least nine children, we learn, because of a traditional need for labor, combined with the high infant mortality rate in Nigeria. *The Desired Number* demonstrates the hardships of women because of this cultural practice. Women are recognized for their efforts with the Ibu Eze ceremony. *The Desired Number* demonstrates that birth control has been misused as a colonializing practice imposed upon African people. A Nigerian nurse, for example, argues that the common use of Depo-Provera, which is an injected form of birth control, implies that African women are too irresponsible to take the Pill or use another type of birth control. A better option, she suggests, is the self-managed family-planning clinic, where women are able to learn about various methods of birth control and make a choice in consultation with their families. Instead of enforcing birth control upon Nigerian women, the West might do better to stay out of the issue and stop sending Christian missionaries who preach against birth control.

Onwurah's ethnographic approach to the women and men of the Iwollo village in *The Desired Number* rejects First World consumption of Third World issues and people. As Poonam Arora reminds us, films that successfully manage to avoid this pattern demonstrate "attention to culturally specific structures of representation" (294), thus avoiding the tendency to characterize African women as disempowered, tradition-bound, weak, passive, and incapable of free thought or action. This is not to say that Onwurah completely embraces cultural difference and disavows her own Western feminism. Instead, she walks between the margins of cultural representation as she exposes them in all of their paradoxes. Most importantly, in both *Monday's Girls* and *The Desired Number*, Onwurah sheds light on the ways in which:

Contact with white societies has not generally led to a more "progressive" change in African and Asian sex/gender systems. Colonialism attempted to destroy kinship patterns . . . disrupting, in the process, female organizations that were based upon kinship systems which allowed more power and autonomy to women than those of the colonizing nation. (Carby 224)

As Hazel Carby comments in *The Empire Strikes Back*, African women's struggle to gain control over their own bodies and reproductive systems has been undermined by intrusive colonial practices, including the invasive "racist experimentation with the contraceptive Depo-Provera and enforced steriliza-tions" (219). *The Desired Number* demonstrates that Nigerian women are tak-ing control of their bodies, by either choosing to remain traditional or opening family planning clinics. *Monday's Girls* celebrates the power and autonomy that young African women gain in the iraye ceremony, and at the same time dia-logically enunciates the manner in which the disruptive forces of colonialism have rendered Asikiye completely unable to take part in the female celebration of power and community, nevertheless she affirms her own Westernized sense of autonomy and pride in this choice. Few ethnographic films articulate the multifaceted experience of Black women across differing systems of economy, kinship, and community.

In 1994, Ngozi Onwurah directed one of the first authentically independent Black British feature films, *Welcome II the Terrordome*. *Welcome II the Terror-dome* is a dystopic political action thriller. Its militancy has come under criti-cism; however, its reception must be read within the context of its ability to disrupt Hollywood films that generally draw upon a "variety of narrative and visual 'strategies of containment' that subordinate the Black image and subtly reaffirm dominant society's traditional racial order" (Guerrero 237). Critics' discomfort with the militancy of *Welcome II the Terrordome* reaffirms the le-gitimacy of the experiences of bell hooks, who also found that her militant writings voiced "ideas many Black folks hold but dare not express lest we ter-rify and alienate the white folks we encounter daily. . . . Black militancy is al-ways too extreme in the white supremacist context, too out-of-order, too dan-gerous" (1994, 359). British critics' discomfort with the film demonstrates a parallel phenomenon in America noted by Henry Louis Gates, Jr., in which Af-rican-Americans have demonstrated a "paradoxical tendency to censure its own" (200). Ngozi Onwurah breaks the binds of the critics who attempt to enforce a gag order of sorts, one that Kobena Mercer dubs the "social respon-sibility of the artist Paradigm" (248). As a member of the Black British com-munity (and the larger diasporic Black community), not to mention the Black women's community, Onwurah flies in the face of the notion of the artist who is assumed, at times to be "racially 'representative,' in the sense of speaking on behalf of a supposedly homogeneous and monolithic community . . . binding him or her ever more closely to the burden of being 'representative.' " (Mercer 248).

Ngozi Onwurah refuses to be a so-called "representative" Black/woman. As she told Trevor Ray Hart, in an interview in *Time Out*, "what they expect a Black woman film-maker to be making is definitely not the kind of movies I want to make" (22). Onwurah readily admits that she has a "different concept and agenda for film-making," and she remarks upon the importance of the fact that her film features "Black women with guns." While traditional action films from Hollywood champion white (or Black) men, with guns, they generally function to remove the dangerous threat of blackness. *Welcome II the Terrordome* disrupts this colonizing signification, and, as Onwurah herself says nothing to assuage anyone's fears, "I don't expect to feel safer walking around because my film was seen by some people" (Hart 19).

Welcome II the Terrordome is a highly disturbing and disrupting call for action. By placing the narrative in the future of a grim dystopic science fiction landscape, Onwurah displaces and rereads Black history. In this way, Onwurah masterfully evokes the past and the present through the scopic prism of the future. The absences of popular memory of colonialist domination of the Black body, and the present Black struggles against drugs, continual racism, unemployment and poverty, are evoked through a multiple chain of associations in the film. *Welcome II the Terrordome* proves that it is possible for "the 'colonized' [to] express an authentic self in an alien language imposed by the imperial power of the colonizer" (Mercer 63). It forces the viewer to confront the Black body as a site of commodification, sterilization and culturally approved genocide. It is unflinching in its exposure of police brutality against Black people that is supported by institutionalized racist theorizations of blackness, which, as Paul Gilroy comments, "legitimate new police tactics and methods for containment of social disorder" (154) and are based on "pathological conceptions of Black life" (153). The most chilling moment comes for the spectator when she/he realizes that the grim science fiction *mise-en-abîme* of the Terrordome is hardly a fiction at all, only a slightly exaggerated simulacrum of reality as it is faced every day by Black people in American cities. It is this unflinching re-vision of reality across the chain of multiple signifiers that is so brilliant in the film. The filmmaker's state of mind when she wrote the film accounts, in part, for its *mise-en-abîme*:

I wrote it in about three days when I had a toothache and couldn't get to the dentist and they put me on painkillers, so I was smashed out of my head, playing Public Enemy in my bedroom, in agony. And what I did was put lots of true stories in—like a white friend of mine who was pregnant by a Black guy, and her ex-boyfriend [who is white in the film version] came and punched the baby out of her, and then there was the Howard Beach incident—and I put all these things together happening to a group of people during one night. (Hart 19)

Welcome II the Terrordome takes its name from the music of the rap group Public Enemy, dragging the politics of hip-hop Hollywood films into direct confrontation with the economy of the Black body. This economy continually reinforces codes that measure the worthiness of bodies according to race and gender. Black women and men are routinely devalued, murdered and sacrificed in Hollywood feature films. The dystopic world of the Terrordome is a city ghetto of the future, where only blacks live and the economy is drug based. Two rival Black gangs fight for business with white customers from outside the city. Angela (played by Suzette Llewellyn) is married to Black Rad (played by Felix Joseph). She tries to shield her son, Hector (played by Ben Wyter), from the drug-dealing life. Black Rad's brother, Spike (played by Valentine Nonyela), is living with a white woman, Jodie (played by Saffron Burrows), who is pregnant by Spike. Jodie's white ex-lover, Jason (played by Jason Traynor), is a vicious racist. One day he sees Jodie with Spike and decides to turn in Spike's gang to the police. He assaults Jodie and kicks her until she begins to miscarry. Meanwhile, Angela's son, Hector, dies trying to flee Jason's gang. Angela shoots Jason and the white cops who try to arrest her. Angela's family turns on Spike and Jodie, blaming them for the death of Hector and the arrest of Angela. Hector's grandmother, Rosa, explodes in a tirade against white people. A voice-over of a Black man explains that he has no pity for the white woman or the fetus. He has only anger. "I want you to be angry with me. I'm sick and tired of going to the funerals of Black men who have been murdered." On the soundtrack we hear excerpts from speeches of Malcolm X:

Until the American Negro lets the white man know that we are really really ready and willing to pay the price that is necessary for freedom, our people will always be walking around here second-class citizens, or what you call, "twentieth century slaves." The price of freedom is death.

Onwurah cuts this extradiegetic speech into the scene of the funeral for Hector. She intercuts it with shots of Black men training to overthrow the government, shots of Jodie in horrible pain, shots of Angela being brutalized by the police on videotape, and an overhead shot of Hector's dead body as it is mourned by his family. The film is steeped in scenes of violence and darkness, in a film that demands a lifting of the veil of suppressed realities, and demands the desensitized viewer to engage in sensitivity, in looking at, and being looked at, by images of unspeakable horror. The unspeakable images include a neck-lacing of a Black man by a rival gang, the brutality that Jodie suffers at the hands of her ex-lover, numerous scenes in which police brutalize Black men and women, the death of Hector, and the horrible, sadistic beating of Angela, who is tied to a chair and tortured by a white woman prison guard. These scenes are particularly horrific, because they are viewed off of the panopticonic video monitor of the police station, and they force us into an admittance of the role of white women in oppressing Black women. In her writings, Alile Sharon Larkin underscores the importance of asking the question, "What about the historical oppression of Black women and men at the hands of white women?" (166). A moment in the opening sequence of the film suggests that Onwurah recontextualizes this question across the span of time, beginning in the seventeenth century, in the roots of slavery.

The opening sequence, the Ibo landing of *Welcome II the Terrordome*, con-fronts us with the sexual politics between white women and African slaves that continues to be played out in a hybridized modern fashion. During the pro-logue, filmed in sepia tones, the Ibo people of West Africa are shackled and chained in leg irons and collars. A captured African slave is dragged to the ground and branded. A colonial woman with a distinctly southern accent says, "Thank heavens they got him. I'm sure I'll sleep better." Another white woman, who is Jodie in the future world, exchanges a sultry look with an African man in shackles. The sexual politics of racism are indelibly grounded in the com-modification of Black bodies, and white women are inescapably significant in this historical and cultural moment. Onwurah avoids the problem of rendering an oversimplified historical narrative by embracing the volatility of the power of the oppositional gaze. In the words of Kobena Mercer, "What made Black Power such a volatile metaphor was its political indeterminacy: it meant dif-ferent things to different people in different discourses" (302).

Reading the signifier of Black militancy in *Welcome II the Terrordome* across cinematic discourse is a hyperrealist act of revisualizing the past and future of Black people. Onwurah embraces the hyperreal (as it is described by Baudril-lard), the narrative of Black bodies floating through time and space, trans-gressing the binaries of subject/object, death/life beyond the codes of the West-ern constructed panopticon projection space. Onwurah's hyperreal not only reaches out to the audience but is manifested in the metaphor of the spiri-tual voyage across liminal time and space. In the prologue of the film, the Ibo people walk into the sea to their spiritual lives. They end up at the Terrordome, and after a lifetime of slavery as drug dealers they finally throw over the white ruling class in an armed uprising. In the final images, Onwurah cuts back to the Ibo landing, where the Africans emerge from the sea and raise their arms to break their shackles. If the price of freedom is death, as the film argues, it must be remembered that according to Ibo legend, "Death is not the end, but the start of a voyage back to the spiritual homeland." If the images of *Welcome II the Terrordome* are sometimes received as unwelcome, it is only further proof of Stephen Greenblatt's assertion that "At the moment . . . Europeans embarked on one of the greatest enterprises of appetite, acquisition, and control in the history of the world, their own discourses became *haunted by all that they could not control*" (my emphasis, xvii).

The Black rage that is routinely contained by mainstream Hollywood hip-hop/gangsta films is fully unleashed in the powerful narrative of *Welcome II the Terrordome*. The film exposes the market economy of drug-trafficking of the modern city of "enclosed illegality" (278), as described by Michel Foucault. In the film, the Terrordome is a metonymic metaphor, at once signifying a prison and the city, where Black men are enslaved in the economy of the drug trade. In the film, the drugs are provided by white drug lords. The police, in turn, "make sure the drugs stay in the ghetto." This schema reflects the rise of drug traffic in Black urban communities, which is contained and monitored by the police who report to the ruling class. The attitude toward the drug trade, like the attitude toward the slave trade, as Michel Foucault explains, springs from the prison organization of enclosed and controlled illegality "of which the poorer classes are often the first victims" (278). This breeds a life of supervised delinquents. The imprisonment of Black people, as in the Terrordome:

. . . cannot fail to produce delinquents. It does so by the very type of existence that imposes upon its inmates: whether they are isolated in cells or whether they are given useless work, for which they will find no employment. . . . it is to create an unnatural, useless and dangerous existence. (Foucault 206)

At the same time, the carceral system "succeeds in making the power to punish [seem] natural and legitimate" (Foucault 301). *Welcome II the Terrordome* is a horrifyingly dystopic glimpse of a carceral society to come, as much as it is an indictment of the carceral society of today and the carceral society of colonial slavery of the past. The carceral colonization of the Black body is monitored by the police through the panopticonic video camera, in which all events are recorded. *Welcome II the Terrordome* evokes the penitentiary system described in Foucault's study of the prison system and studies the politics of the colonial subjugation of Black people. Onwurah turns the panopticonic gaze against itself, and unveils the Black-speaking subject as an agent of self-empowerment. The film's movement across historical time periods "requires the spectator's recognition of the double, or paradoxical, status of moving images that are present referring to events which are past" (Nichols 117). The doubling of temporal zones mediates the filmic knowledge across boundaries of the border zones of realistic narratives. Ngozi Onwurah, in both *Welcome II the Terrordome*, and all of her other films, works within what Bill Nichols terms "the blurred border zones of realism" (119). The cinema of Ngozi Onwurah demands that the participatory viewer engage in embodied knowledge that lies beyond traditional hermeneutic knowable truths. In all cases, we are moved to ask questions beyond the text, we are moved beyond objectivity into subjectivity and left with the desire for introspection. In so doing, Onwurah responds to Homi K. Bhabha's demand that we begin to "open up an intertextual space in between the signposts of traditional inquiries" (1992, 82). Ngozi Onwurah's auto-ethnographic, ethnographic, and (hyper)narrative films move the knowledge of Black corporeality across the boundary of colonialist hegemony. If she incites rage and invokes pain, she does so to indict received notions of passivity and ignorance. Hers is a thinking and feeling cinema, a wedding of formalism and realism and something irreducibly and excessively corporeal and hyper-real.

❖ 4 ❖

JULIE DASH
"I think we need to do more
than try to document history"

How has hollywood filmmaking constructed blackness? Perhaps an even better question is : How has Hollywood filmmaking constructed American whiteness? How do the films of Julie Dash, an African-American woman who is widely regarded as the most successful Black woman filmmaker "working within the system," question Hollywood constructions of American blackness, whiteness, and multiracedness? Julie Dash is a member of a group of Black independent filmmakers known as the LA Rebellion, a group of UCLA graduate students who were "engaged in interrogating conventions of dominant cinema, screening films of socially conscious cinema, and discussing ways to alter previous significations as they relate to Black people" (Bambara 119). First and foremost, the films of Julie Dash take on constructions of whiteness and blackness against the grain of American cinema.

Mark Reid has aptly noted that "film imagery has its roots in slavery," and that Hollywood studios have "portrayed race relations as a static exchange in which all the villains and victims are Black, and all the saviors are White" (1992, 26). The early short films that Julie Dash directed worked to displace Hollywood imagery and replace it with an oppositional cinema of Afrocentricism. In *Diary of an African Nun* (1977), *Four Women* (1978), and *Phillis Wheatley* (1989), Dash rejects the "Klan mentality" that Mark Reid locates in American films, including D. W. Griffith's *Birth of a Nation* (1915) "and its descendants" (1992, 28). Julie Dash's work is a direct response to a cinema that seeks to silence her voice, locate her as an exotic threatening Other, and signify her as "lack" or "absence," both because of her gender and race. *Diary of an African Nun* is an adaptation of a short story by Alice Walker, *Four Women* is an experimental dance film, and the more recent *Phillis Wheatley* is a celebration of the early African-American poet, Phillis Wheatley (1753–84), who is undergoing a renaissance in feminist and post-colonial literary circles.

In 1982, Dash completed *Illusions*, the first in a series of films that deconstruct images of Black women Hollywood films. *Illusions* is set in 1940s Hollywood, and concerns a Black woman who is herself working (as producer) "within the system," though she is "passing" as white. *Daughters of the Dust* (1990) is set at the turn of the century, and Dash plans to set a futuristic film, *Bone, Ash and Rose*, in 2050. Charting and mapping new representations of gendered American blackness and whiteness, this project is a far-reaching re-narration of that which has not been spoken as much as it is a radical commentary on what has been spoken in Hollywood representational practice. As Julie Watson and Sidonie Smith argue, for the colonial subject, "the process of coming to writing is an articulation through interrogation, a charting of the conditions that have historically placed her identity under erasure" (xx).

Illusions interrogates erasure and the political questions around the construction of Blackness and Whiteness in Hollywood films. *Illusions* places the "passing" Black figure, Mignon Dupree, at the center of a construction within another construction. A film within the film self-reflectively points out this constructedness. Dash underscores the necessity of interrogating American films' constructions of Whiteness and Blackness. *Illusions* enacts the critical work forwarded by cultural critic Cornel West. West affirms that Black diasporic women's experience demands that we begin to "examine and explain the historically specific ways in which 'whiteness' is a politically constructed parasitic of 'Blackness' " (213).

Julie Dash's reconfiguration of the Hollywood construct of "passing" calls attention to the phenomena that Toni Morrison calls "American Africanism" (6), or the construction of American whiteness that depends on the denarration of the presence of African-Americans. Morrison describes the process of American Africanism in her study of American literature, *Playing in the Dark*. According to Morrison, it is important to study the signs of American Africanism, the "significant and underscored omissions, startling contradictions, heavily nuanced conflicts, [and] the way writers peopled their work with the signs and bodies of this presence" (6).

Julie Dash's *Illusions* calls attention to a strikingly familiar American Africanist presence in Hollywood cinema. Passing is interrogated in *Illusions* from the inside of the subjective experience of a Black actress and a Black woman director. For the first time, passing is presented from an African-American perspective rather than an American Africanist perspective. Passing, according to Mary Ann Doane, "raises hermeneutical problems of knowledge, identity, and concealment" (234). One way Hollywood erased such hermeneutical problems was to cast white women in roles of African-American women (as passing). Thus issues around concealment and identity were contained, if not erased. *Illusions* not only calls into question issues of identity, but also Hollywood's dependence and referral to psychoanalytic practices that erased Black male and female subjectivity and elided it with white female sexuality as the unknowable "dark continent" (Doane 1991, 211). *Illusions* critiques Hollywood's dependence upon a sex-gender economy that mimics Freudian troping of women's sexuality and Black women as dark continent, and in so doing, throws into question the constructedness of race and sexuality, as well as the constructedness of gender on the American silver screen.

In *Illusions*, Mignon Dupree works as an executive assistant at National Studios, a movie studio that specializes in World War II call-to-arms films and popular musicals. Mignon is placed in charge of supervising the sound-editing of a musical for which a young Black singer, Ester Jeeter, has been hired to overdub a musical voice-over in place of a young white woman. Ester immediately recognizes that Mignon is "passing," and the two women become friends. The film is placed in the historical context of World War II, when Hollywood was fiercely involved in the construction of whiteness, particularly in the white male war hero and the white female object of desire.

Mignon walks through this historic film period, continually gesturing toward the appropriation of nonwhite people in the films of the war effort. The central appropriation is, of course, that of the sexuality in the voice of Ester Jeeter, who is appropriated to construct the female sexuality of the white singer. The practice was quite common in the thirties and forties, and it could be read as a simultaneous erasure of Black female sexuality and an example of the construction of female whiteness. As Patricia Mellencamp comments, Dash reveals "what is repressed by the 'cinematic apparatus' " (79). In constructing the white female, Hollywood musical numbers treated women as substitutable fragmented constructions.

Illusions not only lifts the veil around the construction of white femininity in Hollywood, but it also lifts the veil around the erasure of Native American and Black masculinity through Hollywood mythmaking. In the film, for example, Mignon attempts to correct the historic erasure of the accomplishments of Navaho Marines, who lent their language for an unbreakable code used by the military. Her superior, Lieutenant Bedsford, rejects the idea. At the end of the film, after she has been recognized as African-American, Mignon rails against the erasure of Black men and women:

You see, Lieutenant, I never once saw a film showing "my boys" fighting for this country, building this country . . . your scissors and your paste methods have eliminated my history, my participation in this country. . . . And the influence of that screen cannot be overestimated.

Mignon's outburst decisively ruptures Hollywood mythmaking and its miscegeneic erasure of nonwhite people in the construction of American history. Mignon's outburst has an autobiographical resonance. Having viewed more than 700 films as a member of the MPAA Ratings Administration between 1978 and 1980, Dash was acutely aware of the Hollywood cut and paste methods as they are applied to African-American representation. As Judith Mayne writes, *Illusions* "can be seen as arguing *for* the appropriation of Hollywood film to tell 'other stories,' " while at the very same time it "questions that very assumption" (1990, 62). *Illusions* mimics Hollywood conventions as much as it exposes them. Perhaps one of the most fascinating instances of mimicry is in Mignon's mimicry of white women's constructedness itself.

When the people around her construct her as "white," Mignon is subject to the rules of a white female construct. She has the power and privilege of a white woman, and the white woman's gaze, but she is also subjected to the sexual politics of being objectified as a white woman. When Bedsford views Mignon Dupree as a white female, she is subject to sexual harassment. When she fights for Ester Jeeter's rights, her actions are motivated from her ethos as an African-American woman, however, her power as an executive is built on her White constructed identity. Dash brilliantly evokes Hollywood constructions of femininity that are so often narrated across dualities of identity calling to mind countless films from the forties that engage in such dual identities.

By exposing the constructedness of Whiteness in the central character, Mignon, Dash at once both invites and problematizes cinematic identification. Dragging the viewer into a recognition of identity politics, Dash lifts the veil over the process of identification in an oscillating construction of Mignon between "Whiteness" and "Blackness." The viewer is forced to recognize and confront the fact that:

The process of identification is designed to encourage a denial of one's identity, or to have one construct identity based on the model of the other, mimetically repeating, maintaining the illusion that one is actually inhabiting the body of the ego ideal. (Friedberg 44)

Illusions enables a critique of psychoanalytic theories that tend to erase the Black female spectator. *Illusions* opens up an anti-mimetic space for Black female spectatorship. It is, as bell hooks writes, through "inverting the 'real-life' power structure, [that] Dash offers the Black female spectator representations that challenge stereotypical notions placing us outside the realm of filmic discursive practices. (1993, 300). African-American female spectatorship (like all spectatorship) is fluid, and *Illusions* recognizes this fluidity. Critic Michele Wallace feels a discomfort with the fluidity of her identification as a Black woman spectator. However, Wallace recognizes the politics of her own shifting construction of subjectivity and identity: "As a desiring subject, my coterminous and simultaneous identification with Joan Crawford *and* Hattie McDaniel . . . helped to form the complicated and multifaceted 'me' that 'I' have become" (1993, 264–65).

Of all the tricks and artifices that Julie Dash unmasks in *Illusions,* one that stands out as a rupture of American cinema practice is the illusion of the static frame as a mimetic representation of history. *Illusions* begins to unravel what has been "passing" for American history, what has been "passed off" and constructed as "Whiteness" and "Blackness" in black and white. Dash uses mimicry of Hollywood cinema practice "to show how all representations are constructed, for what purpose, by whom, and with what compliments," taking up the work of cultural critic as it is defined by Edward Said (314).

Illusions acts as a palimpsest: with the doubling of Mignon Dupree, a Black woman working "within the system" and Julie Dash herself, who is an African-American woman director, "working within the system." Many of the statements made by Mignon Dupree resound with significance in light of Dash's work. As Mignon tells Ester, she went to Hollywood because she "wanted to be where history was made where it is rewritten on film." She slowly comes to the realization "There's nothing here for me anymore. . . . There's no joy in the seduction of false images." Yet ultimately, Mignon (and Dash) resolve to stay and fight the system from within. At the end of the film, Mignon tells Bedsford she plans to stick it out:

> I thought there was nothing here for me. I wanted to leave this, this magic carpet we call film. Now I'm going to stay. You fight your war and I'll fight mine. And, if I have to work shoulder-to-shoulder with you to learn everything you know then that's just what I'll do. From now on, Lieutenant, I'm here for the same reasons you are.

Mignon's resolve to fight from within the system is prophetic. For Julie Dash, the fight was only just beginning. The fight to finance and produce *Daughters of the Dust* began in 1986, though Dash began researching and writing *Daugh-*

ters of the Dust in 1983 after finishing *Illusions*. At first, Dash conceived *Daughters of the Dust* as a short film about the struggles of African-American people of the Sea Islands off of North Carolina. Dash elaborates the full story behind her conception of the film in her book, *Daughters of the Dust: The Making of an African-American Woman's Film*. She researched at the Schomberg Center for Research in Black Culture in Harlem, the National Archives and the Smithsonian Institution in Washington, D.C., and the Penn Center in South Carolina. Initially, Dash was motivated by a need to document her own family history; however, she found that when she asked family members about their history in South Carolina "they were often reluctant to discuss it" (5). What began as an auto-ethnographical study began to emerge as a community based ethnographic study, and ultimately moved beyond even these categorizations. In 1985, Dash began to write the first version of *Daughters of the Dust*.

Financing the film involved an extraordinarily lengthy and difficult battle within the system of independent production. Dash secured support from the National Endowment for the Arts, Women Make Movies, Inc., and various other arts organizations. As the film evolved into a full length feature project, Dash completed a demo reel and went to Hollywood to find major studio backing; she was met with resistance in the form racism and sexism. Dash remembers that though Hollywood executives were "generally impressed with the look of the film . . . they could not process the fact that a woman filmmaker wanted to make a film about African-American women at the turn of the century" (8). Finally, in 1988, Dash secured backing from American Playhouse. Production began in August of 1989. After an arduous shoot, Dash began editing the film at her home in January, 1990. She was running out of funds, but she received a Rockefeller Fellowship and a grant from the National Black Programming Consortium for postproduction.

When the film was finished, Dash began looking for distribution. Working within the system took on added difficulties, again based on the racism and sexism of Hollywood production executives. As Dash writes, "I was told over and over again that there was no market for the film. . . . Again, I was hearing mostly white men telling me, an African-American woman, what my people wanted to see" (25).

Dash prevailed, and took the film on the international film festival circuit. The film was critically acclaimed from Sundance, Utah, to Munich, Germany. Finally, in 1991, Kino International of New York decided to distribute *Daughters of the Dust*. *Daughters of the Dust* premiered theatrically at the Film Forum in New York City on January 15, 1992. Julie Dash became the first African-American woman filmmaker to release a feature film in the United States. Despite the critics' tendency to single out her achievement, Julie Dash was quick to point out that she considered herself "one of a community of some very talented, powerful women filmmakers—women such as Neema Barnett, Ayoka Chenzira, Zeinabu irene Davis, and Michelle Parkerson" (26).

The most significant aspect of Julie Dash's storytelling ability in *Daughters of the Dust* is her unique revisualization of history, her use of cinematic devices that blur the boundaries between narrative, documentary, and ethnographic styles of filmmaking. Dash uses a *bricolage* of styles that evokes a multivoiced bridging of visual storytelling traditions. As Dash told Houston A. Baker, Jr., "I think we need to do more than try to document history. I think we need to probe. We need to have the freedom to romanticize history, to say, 'what if,' to use history in a speculative way and create speculative fiction" (163).

Daughters of the Dust challenges Hollywood narrative techniques that typically ignore African-American history, particularly Black women's history. It also challenges documentary and ethnographic approaches that tend to objectify the Black subject as object. Like the performative documentary, the performative narrative of *Daughters* interrogates history and storytelling. In performative documentaries such as *Reassemblage* and *Tongues Untied*:

> Observational techniques no longer give the impression of "capturing" the referential realm itself, the historical world as it is, so much as lend stress to qualities of duration, texture, and experience, often liberated from intimate associations with social actors giving virtual performances according to the expressive codes familiar to us from fiction. (Nichols 95)

In an interview with Greg Tate, Arthur Jafa, the cinematographer and co-producer of *Daughters*, elaborated upon the visual approach in the film:

> At every point we utilized African-American expressivity as an ordering directive. This meant constructing an alternate universe of visual references and cinematic procedures, one in which Black beauty has self-determining agency. (1992, 90)

Daughters of the Dust ritually transforms loss and recovery of personal and public African-American memory. In renarrating the tales of the Gullah at the turn of the century, Dash evokes suppressed signs and sounds of the past. From the beginning of the film, the viewer is presented with a melange of Gullah culture through sounds, images, and performances. It is the attention to the nuances of rituals, styles, and especially the kinesthetics of gesture, which

Zeinabu irene Davis at work in the editing room.
Courtesy Women Make Movies, Inc.

Scene from *A Powerful Thang* by Zeinabu irene Davis.
Courtesy Women Make Movies, Inc.

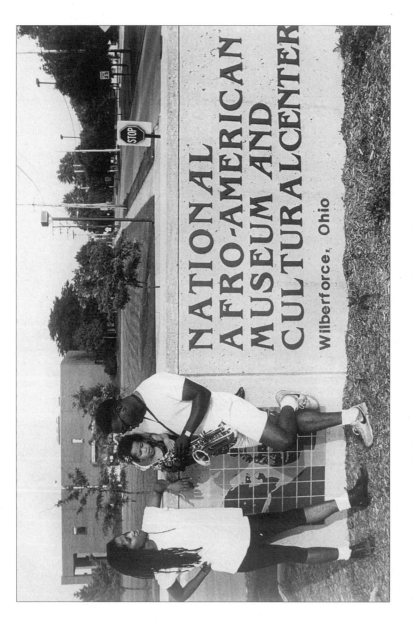

A family outing in *A Powerful Thang* by Zeinabu irene Davis.
Courtesy Women Make Movies, Inc.

Scene from *Mother of the River* by Zeinabu irene Davis. Courtesy Women Make Movies, Inc.

In the nighttime forest in *Mother of the River* by Zeinabu irene Davis.
Courtesy Women Make Movies, Inc.

Scene from *Cycles* by Zeinabu irene Davis. Courtesy Women Make Movies, Inc.

Scene from *Monday's Girls* by Ngozi Onwurah. Courtesy Women Make Movies, Inc.

Sian Martin in *The Body Beautiful* by Ngozi Onwurah.
Courtesy Women Make Movies, Inc.

Scene from *Illusions* by Julie Dash. Courtesy Women Make Movies, Inc.

Scene from *Praise House*
by Julie Dash. Courtesy Women
Make Movies, Inc.

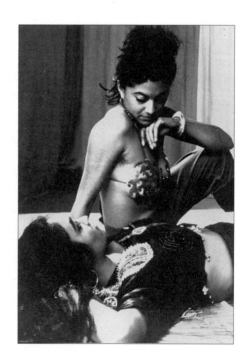

Scene from *Khush*
by Pratibha Parmar.
Courtesy Women Make Movies, Inc.

Scene from *Sari Red* by Pratibha Parmar.
Courtesy Women Make Movies, Inc.

Scene from *Warrior Marks* by Pratibha Parmar.
Courtesy Women Make Movies, Inc.

June Jordan (*left*) and Angela Davis in *A Place of Rage* by Pratibha Parmar.
Courtesy Women Make Movies, Inc.

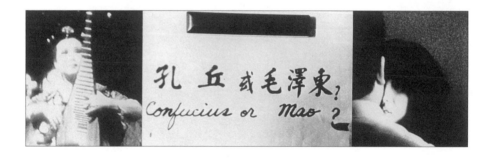

Scene from *Shoot for the Contents* by Trinh T. Minh-ha.
Courtesy Women Make Movies, Inc.

Scene from *Reassemblage* by Trinh T. Minh-ha. Courtesy Women Make Movies, Inc.

Scene from *Naked Spaces—Living Is Round* by Trinh T. Minh-ha.
Courtesy Women Make Movies, Inc.

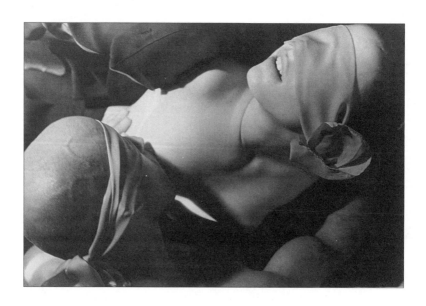

Scene from *A Tale of Love* by Trinh T. Minh-ha.
Courtesy Women Make Movies, Inc.

Scene from *Hair Piece* by Ayoka Chenzira.
Courtesy Women Make Movies, Inc.

Scene from *Perfect Image?* by Maureen Blackwood.
Courtesy Women Make Movies, Inc.

Scene from *Stormé:
The Lady of the Jewel Box* by
Michelle Parkerson. Courtesy
Women Make Movies, Inc.

Scene from *Home Away from Home* by Maureen Blackwood.
Courtesy Women Make Movies, Inc.

strongly evokes an Afrocentric visual memory making. As Dash told Zeinabu irene Davis, she took a particular interest in embodying signs of the survival of African culture in the Gullah people:

> People's motor habits—the way they stand and the way they walk, the way they laugh—I tried to maintain the integrity of West African motor habits. An example would be of turning the head slightly to the left when listening to an elder and putting a hand over your mouth when you laugh. All this is approached from an Afrocentric perspective. I wanted to have a connection to the past. The men have these signals that they give to each other from across the sand dunes. They communicate with one another in hand signals, these were derived from secret societies in West Africa, like the Poro for men and Sande, which was a women's secret society. (116).

The rich cultural signs of embodied memory in *Daughters of the Dust* evoke signs of survival, signs of replacements, signs of loss/absence, and signs of cultural reaffirmation. The African roots of Gullah or "Geechee" culture are signified through images such as the scene of Bilal Muhammed, a Muslim Gullah, reading Koranic verses from a wooden slate, scenes that center around West African style quilts and food, African-derived music, and African hairstyles. Perhaps the most jarring image is the image of a figurehead of an African warrior, that once was attached to the prow of a European slave ship, which floats in the water at the dock of the Ibo landing. Dash included the image after actually seeing such a figurehead in a New York gallery. As she told Houston Baker, "It was huge, monstrous. It struck me as an awful joke that the people who built the ship decided to make the figurehead an African warrior" (165). The figurehead signifies all the horror of the history of the enslavement of African people. The Ibo landing itself evokes the testimony that continues to this day of the Ibo tribespeople who committed suicide by walking into the sea rather than serving as slaves. It is interesting to note that Black British filmmaker Ngozi Onwurah frames her feature film, *Welcome II the Terrordome*, around this same scene of African memory.

Daughters of the Dust is fashioned in a nonlinear construction, however, Dash's thumbnail synopsis of the film, as told to Zeinabu irene Davis, begins to give an approximation of the central narrative:

> It's about a family that's preparing to migrate North and the great grandmother is trying to get them to remain on the island. The story is concerned with conflict and struggle as the family prepares to migrate. . . . These women

carried scraps of memories from the past, and then, they carry these same scraps of memory into the future. (112)

The central woman figure is a widowed great grandmother figure, Nana Peazant (brilliantly played by Cora Lee Day). Her daughter, Viola (played by Cheryl Lynn Bruce), is a Christian missionary. The other central women include Eula (played by Alva Rogers), who is pregnant after being raped by a white landowner. Eula's unborn daughter is the off-screen narrator. Yellow Mary Peazant is played by Barbara-O. Nana Peazant draws upon her spirituality to hold onto her departing family. She is in spiritual battle with Haagar, a member of the family who is leading the Peazant family toward the North and away from the traditions and beliefs of the African-centered Nana. Nana spiritually realigns Eula and Eli who have had their marriage wrecked by a white rape. Nana Peazant performs a ritual that assures Eli that he is the father of the unborn child.

Another important woman figure is Yellow Mary, who has returned to the island after working abroad as a wet nurse and a prostitute. Yellow Mary relates the horrid memory of the death of her baby. The white family she worked for used her as a wet nurse for their children. This is not only a historical reference to this common colonial practice, but, as Toni Cade Bambara argues, it also alludes to Toni Morrison's novel *Beloved* (1987), in which young white rapists suckle the milk of Sethe. Black women's sexuality and fertility was already a theme in Dash's work prior to Morrison's *Beloved*. Dash's short film of 1978, *Four Women*, for example, also rearticulates the history of sexuality of African-American women.

Daughters of the Dust concludes with a regenerative spirit. The Peazant women are tightly bonded despite the legacy of forced sexual involvement with white slavemasters. Even though some of the family decides to go North, Nana Peazant prevents cultural loss by giving the members of the family articles of significance to reinforce traditional customs despite Northern migration. The title of the film alludes to the dust of African cultural memory evoked in Nana Peazant's actions. Zeinabu irene Davis asked Dash about the significance of the title and Dash responded:

It's kind of paraphrasing a passage in the Bible, in Ezekiel which goes, "O ye sons of the dust," and I changed it to daughters of the dust. Dust also implies the past and something that's grown old and crumbling. The whole film is about memories, and the scraps of memories, that these women carry around in tin cans and little private boxes. Everyone's grandparents or old aunts and uncles have scraps of memories—like when you go to an old relative's house and you find boxes with all these little bits of this and that, that have to do with your family. "Scraps of memory" is also taken from a paper that W. E. B. Du Bois wrote about the fact that African-Americans don't have a solid lineage that they can trace. All they have are scraps of memories remaining from the past. I wanted memory to be a central focus of the story. (111)

Dust, as a metaphor for land and memory, is resignified in the film against a tradition of cinematic representations of African-Americans working the "alien land." In an interview with Julie Dash, published in *Daughters of the Dust*, bell hooks observes this significant metaphorical placement in light of "the psychic loss that Black people experienced when we left the agrarian South to move to the industrialized North . . . I mean, how many films do we see where the Black folk are holding dirt in their hands and the dirt is seen as another gesture of our burden?" (Dash 42). Dust is resignified as a celebratory image of promise and memory in the film.

Dust becomes embedded with African memory and knowledge, and the land of the Ibo landing becomes a bridge between African-Americans and Native Americans, both displaced from their homelands through colonialization. In a letter from her Native American lover, Iona is reminded that the land once belonged to the Indian people. The presence of a Native American people in the film prompted bell hooks to observe to Dash that:

the film creates the sense, that there was a historical overlap between ideas about nature, divinity, and spirit in those two cultures that made convergence and contact possible. I think *Daughters* tries to show that something which, however flawed, we have no other cinematic example of. (Dash 49)

Daughters of the Dust marks the filmic landscape as a reimagining of Native American and African-American space. It also offers a revision of Hollywood spatial colonial practices that erase lesbian space. Yellow Mary and her light-skinned traveling companion, Trula, are lovers in the film. Dash told bell hooks that she decided to include the couple when in her research she suddenly realized the omission of bisexual and lesbian partners, "and in developing Yellow Mary's character, I realized that she, as an independent businesswoman would not be traveling alone. In fact, she would have a significant other person" (Dash 66). The recovery of lost images of Black lesbian women has added resonance in light of the inclusion of Yellow Mary in the female validation ritual. Presented to the other women, Eula demands to the women on-screen and off, "if you love yourself, then love Yellow Mary." The validation of Black lesbian space, both on-screen and offscreen, is of major importance in the work of Julie Dash.

In his introduction to *Black American Cinema*, Manthia Diawara comments upon the importance of Dash's use of space and spatial narration in *Daughters of the Dust*:

> In *Daughters of the Dust*, the screen belongs to Black women. At a deeper level, where space and time are combined into a narrative, Julie Dash emphasizes spatial narration as a conduit to Black self-expressivity, a storytelling device which interrogates identity, memory, and Black ways of life. (1993, 14)

Drawing upon her knowledge of kinesthetic dance forms, Dash refashions blackness in African-American bodies on the screen, creating a new temporal spatiality which crosses both the constraints of time and spiritual boundaries. Black bodies move across historical time periods, from the seventeenth century to the present, and they walk across ancestral liminal zones. Ancestral characters are reincarnated and summoned by Grandmother Nana through the use of innovative cinematic camerawork, stretch printing techniques, slow motion, and elliptic poetic meditations of the Black body as it moves through space. Dash recounts her immersion in the work of the legendary Yugoslavian-born Hollywood montagist Slavko Vorkapich, who had a decidedly strong influence on Dash, particularly in her kinesthetic approach to the African-American body. As Dash told Houston Baker, the Soviet-influenced formalist was present when Dash worked for the American Film Institute:

> He was in his late nineties at the time . . . that was a turning point for me; film aesthetics really weren't clicking in at that time until I had seen his presentations and what you could do with film—in terms of movement of the frame, movement within the frame. (157)

Dash began appropriating and refashioning classical Soviet montage techniques into her own unique approach to time, space, and the body. In *Daughters of the Dust*, the highly stylized images of the body in freeze-frames, optical reprinting, and the shot compositions almost always center on the rituals of African-Americans. The pacing of the film, which is leisurely and freed of conventions of time and space, is not unlike that of African films. The formal explorations of Julie Dash point to a feminist aesthetic, or as Teresa de Lauretis terms, a feminist "de-aesthetic":

> From the inscription of subjective space and duration inside the frame . . . to the construction of other discursive social spaces . . . women's cinema has un-

dertaken a redefinition of both private and public space that may well answer the call for "a new language of desire." (1994, 158)

Some critics have accused Julie Dash, in fact, of being overly aesthetic, or of rendering the Black body as too pretty or perfect. Such readings exemplify "the restricted economy of ethnic enunciation" (5), as defined by Isaac Julien and Kobena Mercer. By restricting the economy of Black visual representation, "individual subjectivity is denied because the Black subject is positioned as a mouthpiece, acknowledgment of the diversity of Black experience and subject positions is thereby foreclosed" (Julien and Mercer 5). In a discussion of the aesthetic elements that Dash evokes in *Daughters of the Dust*, Dash told bell hooks, "I mean, if we cannot fully articulate our pain, then we're not allowed to fully articulate our pleasure either" (Dash, 53). *Daughters of the Dust* articulates the pleasure of the body as it revels in African-American Geechee culture. The celebrations revolve around food, beautiful images of elaborately prepared gumbo, crab, and vegetables. The celebratory preparations of clothing and hairstyling are steeped in references to African-derived spirituality and pleasure. As Julie Dash told bell hooks, some audiences were unable to process these images:

> audiences were not used to seeing Black folk in their nice dresses paying homage to their great-grandmother and not working, not being the beast of burden, they were unable to accept it. No matter what, they still wanted to see someone tailing. They could not accept that this family had food because they were able to sustain themselves from what they planted and what they pulled from the sea. (Dash 45)

Dash heightened the images of beauty and sustenance, the pleasure of looking at Black people through her use of cinematic and narrative techniques. *Daughters of the Dust* is shot on Super 35 Agfa-Geveart film stock, "because Black people look better on Agfa" (Zeinabu irene Davis 115). The use of slow-motion, aided by a computer-driven speed aperture control, allows the viewer to engage in the pleasure of images of bonding, spirituality, eating, hairweaving, dancing, and conversing. The Black oppositional aesthetics of *Daughters of the Dust* allow for the remythologization of the Peazant family, who not only embody ethnographic realities but also symbolize spiritual deities from African cosmology, according to James Lowell Gibbs, Jr. Yellow Mary suggests the Goddess Yemanja; Nana Peazant, the Goddess Oshun; and Eli, the God of War, Ogun (Gibbes 82). Dash renders the beauty of the diaspora by mixing the storytelling traditions of African spiritual practice with African-American

Christian traditions. Throughout the film, we see Nana Peazant fixing a conjurer's charm which is made of a mixture of her mother's hair and her own hair. The hair is sewn into a small bag that is tied to a Bible, and Nana Peazant insists which the family members come forward and kiss the charm. The ritual captures the beauty of female creativity and Gullah culture in its simultaneous embrace of Christian, Arabic, Native American, *and* Yoruba-derived beliefs. Nana Peazant not only represents Oshun, but also the Egyptian Goddess Heka-Maat, or Mother of wisdom, law, and giver of words of power. In early matriarchal culture, Heka-Maat was associated with salvation mysteries. Her teachings enabled admission into areas of the afterworld. In the film, Nana enables the Peazant family in their physical and spiritual journey to the North, which, in order to survive, her speech in the film reminds them of the importance of maintaining spiritual and physical bonds: "There must be a bond . . . a connection, between those that go up North, and those across the sea. A connection! We are as two people, in one body. The last of the old, and the first of the new. . . . We came here in chains, and we must survive."

Julie Dash, through her authorial presence, and through the voice of Nana Peazant, celebrates Afrocentric beauty and the persistence of African cultures despite all colonial efforts of suppression and oppression. Specifically, Dash articulates African and African-American women's power as spiritual guide, conjurer, and healer. Dash not only mythologizes African-American spiritualities, but she inscribes herself through the inclusion of her own family mythology, including the recollections of her mother, grandmothers, father and aunts. Significantly, when asked by Zeinabu irene Davis who she most identified with (in the film), Dash chose Myown, the character who leaves the island carrying Nana Peazant's can full of scraps of memory: "She will be the person, the individual, maintaining cultural traditions in the North, the Western world" (113).

Dash's camera-eye is like the all-seeing eye of the African Goddess Oshun and the Egyptian Goddess Heka-Maat, whose gaze was invested with the spiritual power to see-all and to transgress the physical world and move across spiritual worlds. Dash's myth-making gaze has the power to revisualize African-American spirituality and corporeality. Her cinematic magic-making conjures a truth Logos of spirituality that works in opposition to the colonial gaze, which seeks to cinematically construct blackness only as it relates to whiteness, denying the regenerative power of the African-American camera/eye/tongue. In the words of Toni Cade Bambara, *Daughters of the Dust* marks "a more pronounced diasporic and Afrafemcentric orientation" (142). Dash gestures to a new tradition of filmmaking, one that signifies the process of knowing an African female-centered past and future, one that celebrates Black community as much as it celebrates Black diasporic identity.

The importance of celebrating a multiplicity of spiritualities is central in the work of Julie Dash. Dash's short film *Praise House* (1991) centers around African- American spirituality in a young girl, Hannah, her mother and her grandmother. *Praise House* was produced in collaboration with the performance group, Urban Bush Women, whose founding choreographer, Jawole Willa Jo Zollar, choreographed and collaborated on the film. *Praise House* was adapted by Julie Dash from the original stage play of the same name, which was written by Angela DeBord. The film was produced and distributed by Alive From Off Center. *Praise House* is a meditation on African and African-American spirituality narrated through African dance, music, and theatre. The film includes spectacular visions of an allegorical other world of angels and healers who are conjured by the prophetic visions of Hannah and her grandmother. The conflict between modern American urban society and spiritual belief is highlighted by the mother's inability to cope with her gifted daughter and mother within the confines of her grim existence as a dishwasher.

Hannah (played by Viola Sheely) draws crayon pictures of African female spirituality. She is driven by forces outside herself, angels and healers that engage her in performative rituals. Granny (played by Laurie Carlos) is connected to Hannah and her visions. Granny, like Hannah, sees visions of angels and spirits. She sings and testifies and gives praise to the spirits, however, she relates how difficult it was to grow up gifted within a culture that denied her gift and suppressed her spiritual knowledge. Caught between mother and daughter is Mama (played by Terry Cousar), who tried desperately to cope with her daughter's spirituality, though she cannot understand it. She begs God for understanding, demanding to know why she was given such a child.

The embodiment of spiritual gifts in Hannah's character is cinematically rendered with a giftedness not unlike that of Hannah herself. Hannah draws angels and a crayon drawing of an African-American "seer," surrounded by eyes, signifying the female spirit of the Eye-Goddess, the all-seeing, all-knowing one, female strength, and visual traveling across space and time. Hannah is confused, yet enraptured by her own ability to draw. By the end of the film, she conjures a vision of a Bible that has a message written across it: "Draw or Die." She must allow her spiritual visions to come forth. In one scene, Hannah draws colorful auras (rendered by special effects). She plays with angels and healers who come to her at her baptism and take her on a spiritual journey that culminates in a dance at her grandmother's future burial site.

Hair, which plays such a central role in the cultural embodiment of African-American female knowledge in *Daughters of the Dust*, is again centered as a conduit of spiritual knowledge between Hannah and her grandmother. Hannah carefully combs out her grandmother's hair in one scene, and her grandmother tells her that she keeps her secrets in her hair and Hannah learns these secrets by combing out her hair. Hair has significance in a whole range of spiritual metaphors. It is traditionally the bearer of the soul (which is why Nana collects her ancestor's hair and combines it with her hair in a charm in *Daughters of the Dust*). The grandmother is sharing spiritual knowledge with Hannah, the knowledge of peace in the afterworld. Hair, in Western African cultures, was said to embody the spiritworld, just as ancient cultures believed that women used hair to work magic, leading Christian cultures to shave the heads of witches and other spiritual women.

After the hair-braiding scene, Hannah has a vision of a spirit taking her grandmother to another world. She envisions her grandmother's death, but without anxiety. Her mother finds her shivering at the graveyard, and she takes her home. Later, Hannah and the angels dance with the mother and release her pain and anxiety about her daughter's gift and her mother's death.

Hannah's spiritual creativity, like that of Nana Peazant in *Daughters of the Dust*, is uncompromised by modern lack of belief. Indeed, Hannah's message "Draw or Die" is also a message for the African-American woman filmmaker, for African-Americans and for women artists themselves. The importance of self-embodiment through spiritual and artistic subjectivity is perhaps the most important cultural message and embodiment in and of the films of Julie Dash. Like Zeinabu irene Davis, Dash's cinema integrates body and spirit, ontological worlds and spiritual worlds, and reconnects the objectified body with the subjective experiences of African-American women. Julie Dash interrogates what it means to be an African-American woman director, working within the system by insisting that the system be remapped and remade to include the experiences, both physical and spiritual, of American Black women. Dash's women, such as Mignon Dupree, Nana Peazant, and Hanna (of *Praise House*) map themselves onto a cinematic landscape that has consistently erased them in Hollywood Cinema.

❖   5   ❖

PRATIBHA PARMAR
"An assault on racism, sexism, and homophobia"

AS A FILMMAKER, writer, and activist, Pratibha Parmar operates within what Stuart Hall has termed "an oppositional code." Her films embody a zone of signification where "events which are normally signified and decoded in a ne-gotiated way begin to be given an oppositional reading" (Hall 103). Parmar, a lesbian Kenyan-born Indian Black British activist, describes herself within an oppositional reading. In *Queer Looks: Perspectives on Lesbian and Gay Film and Video* (which Parmar co-edited with Martha Gever and John Greyson), Parmar speaks out against overdetermined identity politics that describe her as "mar-ginal," or "other." Parmar states, "I do not speak from a position of marginali-zation but more crucially from the resistance to that marginalization" (5). Par-mar's films move within a sphere of oppositional readings of homosexuality, gender, class, race, color, and a diverse range of issues and identities.

Pratibha Parmar began working in film and video in the early 1980s though she had already been very much involved as a writer/activist as early as the late 60s and early 70s. Unlike many other filmmakers, Parmar stresses her politics were not formed in art school or film school but out of personal experience:

> Since my arrival in England in the mid-sixties, it has been a constant challenge and struggle to defy those institutions and cultural canons which seek repeat-edly to make me believe that because of my visible difference as an Asian woman I am an "other" and therefore "marginal." (5)

In the mid-sixties, British racism toward Black and Indian families was palpa-ble and constant. Many Anglo people refused to accept ex-colonial subjects as individuals. According to Parmar, daily " 'Paki-bashing' was a popular sport amongst white youths" (5), in, for example, Parmar's own school playground. In her early work as a publisher and an activist, Pratibha Parmar recognized and criticized racism, sexism, and homophobia. As one of the founding mem-bers of Black Women Talk, the first Black women's publishing house in Britain, Parmar attacked racism through a "guerrilla" poster campaign designed to end

73

"Asian bashing." The group gained visibility with a poster which depicted a young Asian woman warning: "If anyone calls me a Paki, I'll bash their heads in." The poster itself was emblazoned with the politically charged message: "Self-defense—Not A Sport But a Necessity." Parmar's oppositional political aesthetic was already obviously well formed before she began to use the cinema as a forum for political action. The use of the confrontational "look back," the oppositional gaze of the activist Asian lesbian woman that would become an authorial signature for Pratibha Parmar, is already apparent in this poster. The look back, in which the objectified "other" takes on an active subjectivity and gazes back at the viewer, transgresses the traditional signification process. The women in the poster gaze and interrogate the viewer, who becomes subject to the oppositional gaze. This look back in cinema is one in which the "gaze and the spectator become inverted" (Parmar 10). It is a post-modern strategy that answers Gayatri Spivak's seminal essay question "Can the Subaltern Speak?" with a resounding yes!—and "she" can also confront colonialist forces. By appropriating the apparatus that has been used to colonize and subject her, the Asian Black British woman confronts the viewer.

After working as a researcher for a series of documentaries produced by Britain's Channel 4, Pratibha Parmar was commissioned to direct several films for "Out on Tuesday," a series dedicated to the presentation of gay, lesbian, and bisexual issues. In *Reframing AIDS* (1987), *Memory Pictures* (1989), *Flesh and Paper* (1990), *Khush* (1991) and *Double the Trouble, Twice the Fun* (1992), Parmar turned her oppositional gaze on the politics of heterosexism, racism, essentialism, and other forms of discrimination, including the oppression of people with AIDS and the physically challenged. Parmar was able to move across borders of prescribed identity politics only after she began to question the reinforcement of proscribed "territories" determined by essentialist fixed identity tags. As Parmar recounts, when she began making *Reframing AIDS*, she asked herself:

> What was I, an Asian lesbian, doing making a video about AIDS that did not have just Black women's voices, but also the voices of Black and white men? Why had I dared to cross the boundaries of race and gender? Underlying this criticism was the idea that as an Asian lesbian filmmaker, my territory should be proscribed and limited to my very specific identities, and to my "own" communities. (9)

Parmar states that crossing the boundaries of essentialist identity politics is warranted and necessary because such categorizations act in a manner that is "divisive, exclusionary, and retrogressive." While she agrees that specific identities are necessary as locations of "self enunciation," she adds, "we need them in a political and theoretical discourse on identity which gives us the space for diversity of our imaginations and visions" (9). In Parmar's later film, *A Place of Rage* (1991), June Jordan, Angela Davis, and Alice Walker underscore the political ties between communities of people of color and gay/lesbian and bisexual communities. June Jordan, for example, describes her experience of attending two rallies in one day: one against racism and one against homophobia. Jordan concludes that there must be a "reciprocity" between and across activist struggles, against racist and homophobic violence. In other words, there ought to have been one rally. Pratibha Parmar's radical deconstruction of identity politics challenges the politics of race as they relate to lesbian identity:

> One of my concerns as a filmmaker is to challenge the normalizing and universalizing tendencies within the predominantly white lesbian and gay communities—to assert the diversity of cultural and racial identities within the umbrella category of gay and lesbian. There is a need also to redefine "community," and just as there isn't a homogeneous Black community, similarly there isn't a monolithic lesbian and gay community. (9)

In *Emergence* (1986), an early experimental video that Parmar made with the Black Audio Film Collective, Pratibha Parmar was already challenging the political boundaries of identity, gender, and sexuality. *Emergence* is a performative documentary that interweaves the diasporic voices of four women of color; Audre Lorde, Mona Hatoum, Sutapa Biswas, and Meiling Jin. Transporting diasporic identities across a hostile landscape of white noise, silence, alienation, and fragmentation, *Emergence* moves toward the reintegration of speaking, performing subaltern subjects. The video opens with a montage of images of collective alienation; slides of tropical storms, a shot of a television monitor sending its dismal images out into an empty room; a shot of a shrouded figure encased in black gauze, and a shock cut to a close-up of the eyes of an Asian woman who looks at the viewer, turns away, and then gazes back with an unmistakably challenging look, the gaze of the "other," herself "othering" the viewer. This brilliantly composed juxtaposition of images is manipulated by speed aperture control to evoke a displacement of narrative time and space. The soundtrack (by Trevor Mathieson) assaults the viewer with the unmistakable sound of white noise, the noise we hear in between radio stations or the sound of a television that is not "tuned in," the noise of the unknown space and time continuum. A voice-over begins reading a performative poem:

> Emergence. Personal fragmentation has a collective beginning in the vast landscapes of barren mountains. The diaspora dance continues within its world movements, abrupt dislocations, violent movements. Yet there remains the flame of inspiration to live out joyful visions.

A female disembodied authorial voice-over becomes embodied through the performative sequences, which are intercut with one another, transgressing the boundaries of narrativity and corporeality. Performance artist Mona Hatoum speaks of the alienation she has experienced as a Palestinian woman. Meiling Jin testifies to her experience as an Asian woman who comes from a community of migrant colonialized people who were used as indentured laborers and felt as "strangers in a hostile landscape." Audre Lorde performs her poetry: enacting, reenacting, and transforming personal testimony against a history of silence and invisibility. Sutapa Biswas speaks through the language of her performative body and gaze, interrogating the viewer and rupturing the white noise/(whiteness) that has served to silence the subaltern. *Emergence* is a performative multi/voiced and multi/enacted ritual visual poem that moves women of color, as the voice-over states, "from yesterday's silence to tomorrow's dreams." Woman as speaking subject, gazing subject, interrogating corporeal performative subject owns spatiality in an arena that once depended upon her invisibility, her silence, and the suppression of her performing body. *Emergence* works to recover subjected forms of knowledge. Parmar invokes a performative ethnographic to move across the landscapes of colonial division, in the process underscoring the need for an "ethnographic ear," as defined by Anglo-Asian cultural critic Jenny Sharpe. Sharpe finds that ethnographic listening "exists between and not within cultures . . . beside every native voice is an ethnographic ear" (20).

In fact, *Emergence* demands performative diasporic identities to integrate in defiance of fragmentation. In an interview with Trinh T. Minh-ha, Pratibha Parmar raised the issue of fragmentation, asking a question that is central to any post-colonial debate, "Are we victims of fragmentation or, precisely because of our cultural hybridity and post-colonial experiences of displacement and marginality, are we a synthesis placed very much in the center? "(Minh-ha 1992, 156). Trinh T. Minh-ha's answer speaks to the performative nature of fragmentation in *Emergence*. "Fragmentation is here a useful term because it always points to one's limits. . . . By working on one's limits, one has the potential to modify them. Fragmentation is therefore a way of living at the borders" (Minh-ha 1992, 156–57).

Pratibha Parmar works at the borders of difference with a consciousness of the politics of fragmentation of the experiences of women of color and people of difference. *Emergence* performs and embodies "forms of oppositional con-sciousness, which when kaleidoscoped together comprise a new paradigm for understanding oppositional activity in general" (16), to borrow a phrase from Chela Sandoval. Nowhere is this embrace of oppositional consciousness more apparent, perhaps, than in Parmar's powerful examination of racial violence, *Sari Red* (1988).

Sari Red is made in memory of Kalbinder Kaur Hayre, an Asian woman who was murdered in a racially motivated attack in 1995. In the incident, three White men ran down three Asian women on the sidewalk. Parmar chose not to reenact the horrifying event, leaving the viewer to contemplate the meaning of such a hate crime and the specter of the assault within the mind's eye. As Bill Nichols accurately observes:

> *Sari Red* locates the incident, associatively, within a nexus of class, race, nation, and memory, and the film's poetic/expressive/conative work is less directed at proving what "really happened" than in reframing what has been remembered, contextualizing it within a situated response of memory and collective af-firmation. (99)

Sari Red shares with *Emergence* an eloquence of the performative visual poem. Both films act as films of memory, presenting signs of violence, signs of survival, and signs of agency. In *Sari Red*, Parmar evokes a violent racist attack through the visual repetition of an image of blood as it is splattered on a brick wall. Blood and its color, red, act as shifting signifiers that at once connote memory of what "must not be forgotten," racist sexist violence. At the same time, red and blood denote positive images of the survival of Indian cultural traditions, traditions that celebrate red as the color of India, of the Great God-dess of India, of "the very essence of energy, of joy, of life itself" (Erikson 13). Red is the color of women, the color of femininity, the color of the clothing of Indian women, the sari.

Sari Red opens with a grim spectacle of blood intercut with a montage of memory images, including a statue of the Great Goddess of India, a British flag burning, a red sari, and a close-up of an Indian woman's gaze. In a stylistic gesture similarly used in *Emergence*, *Sari Red* relies upon the enunciative word of a female disembodied voice-over who reads this poem:

Death against the wall.
Blood on the street.
Staining, flowing, marking.
Cannot be erased.
Must not be erased.
Blood,
Cherry red, blood,
Plum red, blood,
Sari red, blood,
Your blood, our blood.

Blood conjures violence against Asian women's bodies as much as it signifies testimony to violence against all Asian people, and people of the international diasporic community. It also evokes violence against the Goddess, the sacred female, the creatrix, the symbol of Asian spirituality and sexuality, the "*sakti*" force from Indian cosmology, which, among many things, signifies the power of logos, as *sakti* can "refer to the capacity of a word generally to possess and convey signification" (Pintchman 105). *Sari Red* acts in a performative arena of "signs of resemblance," as defined by anthropologist David MacDougall who comments that these signs "offer a looser, iconic link with their objects, filling in the missing pattern of the past by analogy" (1994b, 262). The signs of *sakti* in *Sari Red* restore the authority of its signification, for "sakti means power" (Klostermaier 143).

The performative enunciation of *Sari Red* moves across a broad range of associative resemblances, marking off a multitude of metaphoric and metronomic levels of visual language. The pregnant signifier of blood is sutured to images of a pool of blue (and sometimes red) water seen throughout the film. Blue water is another symbol of female life-giving forces. It is also associated with the Great Goddess, and it can resemble both creative and destructive forces. In artwork and religious iconography, the creatrix is often surrounded by blue water, as a representation of the fostering element of the feminine; however, as the destructive force of the universe, she is often seen standing in a sea of blood. As the film unfolds, Parmar cuts back and forth to the pool of blood, which became a pool of blue water, and the Anglo-Asian women move from silence to speaking positions. Here Parmar interweaves images from demonstrations of the Greenwich action against racist attacks and the Southall Black resistance. The voice-over speaks the body of the women of the "Sari Squad": "Daughter. Sister. Friend. She was just 18. She who brought laughter and joy. What were your hopes and dreams for tomorrow? What dreams did you dream?"

The viewer is subjected to grim black and white stock footage that testify to the colonialization of migrant South Asians who were pressed into low-paying factory jobs in England. The voice-over reminds us of the institutionalized racism of labor in Britain. "Our parents came searching for gold. Streets paved with gold, they were told that to entice them." The silent and objectified historical Indian subject stares at the viewer, in defiant opposition to Anglo-Asian history. *Sari Red* draws parallels between the history of South Asian women in Britain as the silent subjects of colonial films and as the silent subjects of immigration legislation and labor practices. Through the mediation of images in the *mise-en-abîme*, these larger issues are unequivocally tied to the murder of Kalbinder Kaur Hayre. Pratibha Parmar, however, repositions silence and absence with activism and voice. The voice-over intones, "We are no longer silent exiles. We watch, looking on, our eyes glimmering through the smoke. Breaking the silence," as we watch images of peaceful Anglo-Indian demonstrations and community organizing.

Sari Red uses the sign of the sari itself as a metaphor for community, agency, testimony, and Asian women's power of resistance. Many times throughout the film a sari is folded and unfolded, and at one point ritually wrapped around one South Asian woman by another, as the oral history of the racist murder of Kalbinder Kaur Hayre is repeatedly enunciated and signified. The tale is thus situated within the folds of the sari as female wisdom, or *sakti*; raw power, both cosmogonic and cosmologic. The choice of the red sari as a location of female knowledge, memory, and empowerment is particularly important, given the cultural importance and history of the sacred sari, the temple cloth of the Mother Goddess and the cloth of all Asian women. As Joan Erikson writes, in her study of the sacred red sari, "Such an object is the pachedi of the Mata, the cloth of the mother goddess, the goddess of a hundred names and as many attributes—that prevailing deity of India since time immemorial" (4).

Sari Red articulates the voice of the Indian Goddess when she is summoned as an icon of female power and the power of the female gaze. The returned gaze of the angry, mourning Asian activists are reenacted by the returned gazes of three dolls hung from a tree, which represent the three women who were brutally attacked. The solemn inanimate stare of the dolls appropriates the male colonializing looks at the viewer, demanding audience involvement. Parmar intercuts between the dolls' eyes, the Indian woman's eyes, and the eye-motif woven into the fabric of the sari. The all-seeing eye is a performative and collective image of female agency. The scrutiny of Anglo-Indian women is tantamount to the omniscience of the Great Mother Goddess, Mata, who is inscribed in the sari. A sari maker, as Joan Erikson comments, would remind you that "the Mata will notice what the average person cannot see" (27). So too, the stare of opposition sees what some cannot see. Yet the omniscient gaze of opposition can also be read as a location of healing and ritual memory-making. The voices and gazes of female colonial subjects resist further erasure and silencing. "She shouted back," the voice-over repeatedly states, referring to Kalbinder Kaur Hayre, to whom *Sari Red* is dedicated. Through performative visual poetics, Kalbinder continues to shout back and look back through the eyes of the activists and the eye of the filmmaker. The look back is a postmodern appropriation of what Parmar cites as one of the "tools of the master" (10). Parmar's use of the "look back" (Dixon 7) in *Sari Red*, and in her subsequent film, *Khush*, is a significant "strategy of appropriation," which Parmar herself cites as a "powerful weapon" in "an assault on racism, sexism and homophobia" (10). Pratibha Parmar's persistent use of the look back, as it is embodied in the South Asian lesbian gaze, moves the borders of the film frame that seeks to "contain" knowledge. As Vivian Sobchack argues, a film's look back represents a signifying subject, not a contained subject, but "a dialogical and dialectical engagement of two viewing subjects. . . . Both film and spectator are capable of viewing and of being viewed, both are embodied in the world as the subject of vision and object of vision" (23).

Pratibha Parmar's *Khush* (1991) stakes out an exchange of lesbian gazes, both between and within South Asian women, on-screen and off. Like Sheila McLaughlin's postmodern lesbian film, *She Must Be Seeing Things* (1987), *Khush* constructs forms of lesbian gaze exchange through the use of a film within the film. In *Khush*, two South Asian lesbians watch a black and white film featuring women in a classical dance sequence. Parmar states, "In the original film, the female dancer's act is intercut with a male gaze, but for *Khush* I reedited this sequence and took out the male gaze" (10). In McLaughlin's *She Must Be Seeing Things*, Jo and Agatha also view a film within a film, displacing the male gaze. Both films make lesbian representation and self-representation possible. As Teresa de Lauretis concludes of McLaughlin's film:

> . . . by addressing the spectator in the place of the desubjectivized subject looking on the fantasy it represents . . . recast and reframed symbolically as a lesbian fantasy—McLaughlin's film does not merely portray a lesbian fantasy . . . but effectively constructs a scenario of lesbian spectatorial desire and en-

ables the visualization—it would be appropriate to say the invention—of a lesbian subject of viewing. (1994, 99–100)

Pratibha Parmar invokes lesbian subjectivity within a celebration of khush subjectivity and identity, invoking the shared experience of being queer and of color. As Parmar appropriates the heterosexual male gaze of the cinema, South Asian lesbians and gays, according to Nayan Shah, "have appropriated the Hindi and Urdu word *khush*, which means happy; some have refigured it to mean 'gay,' while others define it as 'ecstatic pleasure' " (114). Pratibha Parmar explores the global subjectivity of South Asian queer identity, an identity that "has fought silence and invisibility to emerge" (Nayan Shah 114). *Khush* defies the traditional heterosexist and colonialist practice of exoticizing, objectifying, or explaining South Asian queerness in another deliberate move toward identity making. *Khush*, like *Flesh and Paper* (1990), *Memory Pictures* (1989), and *Reframing AIDS* (1987), was made for the lesbian/gay television series, "Out on Tuesday," which was designed "not to explain lesbians and gays to a straight audience. It was very much on the terms that lesbians and gays would do it for themselves" as Parmar stresses in an interview with Khush, the Toronto-based queer South Asian group (Khush Collective 38). For the film, Parmar recorded interviews with members of Asian lesbian/gay/bisexual activist groups including Shakti, in London; Trikon, in California; and Khush, in Canada. On-camera interviews include the polyglossic subjectivities of Punam Khosla, Shivanda Khan, Maya Chowdry, Mita Radhakrishnan, Kartikeya, Kalpana, Poulomi Desai, D. Dalip, Rani Dutt, Mohammed Aslam, Sonia Jabbar, and Giti Thadani, all self-described khush from many different countries and communities. In its multivoicedness, *Khush* avoids flattening, essentializing, or de-privileging multiple South Asian lesbians/gays and bisexuals who may share commonalties, but who, nevertheless, retain individual subjectivities.

The uniqueness of Parmar's ability to document lesbian/gay and bisexual subjectivity while neither sensationalizing, nor normalizing, is underscored by the testimony of many of the speakers in *Khush*, who relate the experience of being objectified, both by the colonial heterosexist community, and the lesbian/gay community. As one woman states, "I've had the experience myself. You are a desirable Oriental, an exotic person to bed with, and you're not recognized as a human being with all the facets that we have." Several people in the film note how racism and classism fragment the lesbian/gay community. White lesbian/gay/bisexual organizations, they argue, all too often ignore the South Asian gay/lesbian/bisexual community, as well as other queer people of color. A gay man who lives on the subcontinent speaks about the need to break down the caste/class system in India that works against a community of solidarity among South Asian khush. Another man locates the centrality of marriage as one unique facet of South Asian culture that oppresses gay/lesbian/bisexual identity. "Due to racism," he explains, "our communities tend to be conservative. Marriage is seen as integral to the maintenance of community." An Asian man or woman is generally forced to come out alone, with little community support and with the crushing obligation to marry.

As one Asian lesbian activist explains in the film, the pressure to marry is so intense that she even considered a "cover" marriage as a means of maintaining her ties to her family and community. Her description is a testimony of the painful decision-making process she went through: "I felt schizophrenic. I felt like there was a part of me that had for four years lived happily as a lesbian." She finally realized the impossibility and self-negating aspects of such an arrangement, but her testimony demonstrates the cultural reinforcement of heterocentricism through the monitoring of familial and community ties. Later in the film, she explains that she concluded that she must "stand up and be counted," as part of the gay/lesbian/bisexual South Asian community. Her speech promotes activism through her enunciation and her self-proclaimed identity:

> I'm a middle-class woman, but I really feel like I must extend myself beyond my experience . . . not just protecting my privilege is crucial . . . we have to do that to expand and make our movement brilliant. . . . Everything is possible for us if we are really committed.

Khush not only locates the shared experiences of cultural isolation of South Asian gays/lesbians and bisexuals, but it also revels in the joy and beauty of khush sexuality and subjectivity. Parmar remakes cinematic pleasure across the spectrum of khush sexualities and the ripe iconographic history of khush sexuality in traditional scriptures, sculpture, and temple art. The pleasures of sexuality are inscribed in the opening testimonies of several South Asian women. One woman states, "the best thing for me about being a lesbian is total erotic satisfaction and endless possibilities." Another says, "Everything about being a lesbian makes me happy. It just fills me, I mean, I'm just filled with the joy of living. It's given me so much strength, this identity. And that strength is what keeps me going."

These bliss-filled descriptions of lesbian *jouissance* mobilize the energies of self- inscribed lesbian subjectivity as much as they locate khush within a tradition of sexuality in India. In India, sexuality and homosexuality are culturally far different from European cultures. Sexuality is an energy in Indian culture, more than a simple physical act. Before colonialism forced the (re)construction of heterosexuality from a European Christian perspective, sexual iconographic displays of same-sex unions and multiple sexual configurations were commonly revered as deities alongside representations of shakti, active feminine strength. As noted in the film, British colonizing soldiers destroyed such images in temples in the eighteenth and nineteenth centuries. However, much of this iconographic testimony is being uncovered by lesbian feminist historians. Homosexuality, pansexuality, and bisexuality are embedded in Indian culture in music and in a culturally rich tradition of the celebration of erotic energies that prevail in modern South Asian culture.

Pratibha Parmar reclaims erotic energies through the testimony of the subjective khush speakers and through the intercutting of images of a loving/gazing Asian lesbian couple. The tableau vivant of the couple is a framing device that serves to encode the film within a sexually charged lesbian gaze. The couple "meet" through a screened panel, representing perhaps, the veil of silence that cloaks the Asian lesbian/gay community. The couple negotiate the space around the screened panel that dissolves into the film-within-the-film. The women in the tableau vivant (played by Rita Wolf and Anna Ashby) own lesbian subjectivity. They gaze at one another, gaze at the audience, and stroke one another. All are acts of lesbian pleasure within a lesbian space. Parmar also encodes this postmodern lesbian scene with a multiplicity of iconographic signifiers of lesbian/gay/bisexual pleasure. A dance sequence, performed by Juanito Wadhwani, is a postmodern performance perhaps of Ardhanarishwara, an Indian mythological figure who embodies the existence of both male and female sexual principles within one body. Wadhwani's erotic dance is intercut with the tableau vivant as he gazes at the audience. This traditional dance performs a ritual celebration of homosexual pleasure and power. These images, in turn, are linked to those of temple carvings that depict women engaged in sexual, spiritual play. The symbol of lesbian sexuality, the lotus (connotative of the female yoni, the feminine life-principle and goddesses such as Cunti, Lakshmi, Padma, and Sakti), makes a frequent appearance in *Khush*.

The lotus, as invoked by Parmar, represents the potential for political agency within the khush community. These erotically charged images are underscored by a lush soundtrack and also interspersed with images of realism that embody same-sex liaisons of sexual pleasure, friendship, and community making. For example, Parmar includes a long take of two men "spooning" in a public park that takes pleasure into the public arena, appropriating and redefining space, in the same way that the tableau vivant at the center of the film remakes lesbian space. Remarkably, Pratibha Parmar, in *Khush*, reproduces lesbian and gay subjectivity without conflating desire and identification. *Khush*'s subjects are at once dialogic configurations of same-sexuality and individual subjects with unique identities and agendas. What is at stake in Pratibha Parmar's *Khush* is what Judith Mayne describes:

> the articulation of lesbian authorship as a critical exploration of the very components of subjectivity: self/other relations, desire, and—where lesbianism provides the most crucial challenge to theories of the subject—the relationship between the paradigms of gender and agency. (1995, 199)

Khush elicits levels of representation and self-representation by reframing lesbian spectatorial pleasure and identity through the primal fantasy of the film-within-the-film. Just as Teresa de Lauretis observes in the case of Agatha and Jo in *She Must Be Seeing Things*, Rita Wolf and Anna Ashby "signify the spatial and representational distance of the spectators from the screen and of the voyeur from the scene looked on" (1994, 99). Pratibha Parmar continually politicizes spectatorial admission by making the viewer highly aware of subject-object relations. At the same time, in the words of Chris Straayer, Parmar opens up spectatorial pleasure "within a new operation of subjectivity in which active desires, pleasure, and other specific declarations of identity construct a field of multiple entry points" (356). Welcoming points and distancing effects characterize Parmar's work. As Parmar herself writes, "I attempt to enunciate the nuances of our subjectivities in my work" (10). *Flesh and Paper* (1990), for example, challenges theories and practices of identification with a refusal to denote its subject, poet Suniti Namjoshi, as "lesbian" at the beginning of the film. As Pratibha Parmar said in her interview with the members of the Khush Collective: "We are lesbians and gays and it's not a problem for us. If it's a problem for others, they have to look at or read our work on our terms" (Khush Collective 39).

In *Flesh and Paper*, Parmar again intercuts an image of a female South Asian classical dancer who symbolizes the poet's erotic subjectivity. Using such an image is a statement of Parmar's cultural authority. As Parmar relates, in a round-table discussion with Joy Chamberlain:

> I've had a variety of criticisms about that, ranging from people saying "You're in danger of presenting an exotic image. You're replicating a particular exoticization of Asian women, in the way she looks and the fact that she's dancing

and being alluring." I don't see her as an exotic image but as a particular icon coming from my particular cultural background. (60)

Flesh and Paper presumes lesbian identity and lesbian authorship in both gaze and subjectivity. Suniti Namjoshi reads from her poems, fables, and novels in the film. Similarly, photographer Sunil Gupta articulates himself and his homosexual subjectivity in *Memory Pictures* (1989), through the gaze of his photographs. With *Double the Trouble, Twice the Fun* (1992), Pratibha Parmar moved her identity politics into an examination of the subjective experiences of physically challenged homosexuals. The film revolves around the central importance of mirror images in the identity-making process. A voice-over narrator opens the film with the statement: "We all need mirrors. . . . Some of us are shy of mirrors, some of us have never had them."

Double the Trouble, Twice the Fun recovers the image-making of lesbian/gay and bisexual disabled individuals. For example, in the film, writer Firdhaus Kanga seeks and finds a mirror image and thus an access to his own identity formation. Typical of Parmar's work, the film deals with difference issues without patronizing or marginalizing the subjects in the film. *Double the Trouble, Twice the Fun* renarrates the suppressed and distorted images of the physically challenged as they have been constructed in images of classical mainstream narrative film.

Either completely omitted or constructed as "lack," and "absence," physically challenged subjects have been fashioned as a nonpresence in Hollywood films. As Mary Ann Doane writes, the clinical gaze of medical discourse films constructs physically challenged people as hysterics. Like Hollywood representations of women, physically challenged people tend to be fashioned as "both socially devalued or undesirable, marginalized elements which constantly threaten to infiltrate and contaminate that which is more central, health or masculinity" (Doane 1987, 38). Pratibha Parmar works toward deconstructing the Hollywood/clinical gaze that distorts the image of disabled subjects. *Double the Trouble, Twice the Fun* reclaims subjectivity and the mirroring Other.

Mirror images of the physically challenged have been routinely constructed as the Other who is undesirable and who represents the threat of lack, loss, or absence. The narrative of the Other is a tale that Mas'ud Zavarzadeh describes as that which "suppresses another tale—the tale that the overt one prevents being told" (19). Parmar renarrates the denarrated tales of the lesbian/gay/bisexual physically challenged, offering an Irigarayan mirroring of the subject that is necessary for "the mastery of the image, of representation, and of self-representation" (Irigaray qtd. in Doane 1987, 15). Thus, subjects who have been denied agency, self-representation, and access to images of autoerotic pleasure and sexual desire emerge in *Double the Trouble, Twice the Fun* as reconfigurations and self-configurations of alterity. The performing subjects in Parmar's film work: "subvert the fetishism of early cinema . . . the object of a medical-cinematic gaze that unveils and analyzes, rises from the dead to denounce her own condition and to reclaim her place and desire" (Bruno 276).

Double the Trouble, Twice the Fun inverts the traditional relationship of the gaze of the spectator. The film clearly rejects classical Hollywood films that relegate people with disabilities to the status of outsider looking in, and replaces this paradigmatic framing device with subjects looking out and looking at self-constructed mirror images. Politically, what is at stake in film enunciation and subjectivity formation is not only control of language but also control of the image and the image-making process. Pratibha Parmar appropriates the conventional testimony of "talking heads" for *Double the Trouble, Twice the Fun*, however, the conventional becomes politicized in the film. As Pratibha Parmar herself comments: "Talking heads can be transgressive if they belong to individuals who have never been given the space on prime time television" (Chamberlain 49).

Like *Khush* and *Double the Trouble, Twice the Fun*, *A Place of Rage* (1991) includes the oral testimony of those who have not been heard, specifically Black lesbian women who renarrate the untold tale of Black women in the Civil Rights movement. In *A Place of Rage* the oppositional talking heads of June Jordan, Angela Davis, Trinh T. Minh-ha, and Alice Walker transgressively retrieve history. Intercut within their multiple narration are elements of the performative documentary, such as images of Jordan, Davis, and Walker running outdoors in public places, owning those spaces from which they have been denied access and ownership. *A Place of Rage* is a rhetorically sophisticated blending of many hybridized documentary forms including talking heads, archival footage, and nonstaged performative images, underscored by music by Prince, the Staple Singers, Janet Jackson, and the Neville Brothers. The suppressed histories of African-American women such as Rosa Parks, Septima Clark, and Fannie Lou Hamer are recounted in the film, which reassesses the Civil Rights Movement within a discussion of the role of the Black Panthers, United States imperialism and involvement in Desert Storm, and the relationship between homophobia and racism in America.

The title of the film refers to June Jordan's account of unprovoked police brutality against people of color, lesbians, and gays. Jordan specifically refers to her experience as a young woman who saw the aftereffects of a brutal police beating on the face of a young African-American boy who lived in her apartment building. He was beaten, Jordan remembers, to the point of disfiguration (for absolutely no reason but racism) by police who supposedly mistook him for a wanted criminal. "It hardened me in a kind of a place of rage," Jordan explains.

A Place of Rage moves the personal narrative, such as the one above, from the margins of discourse, to the center of the history of the African-American in/and the Civil Rights movement. As ethnographer Renato Rosaldo writes, "Although personal narratives often appear in ethnographies in the classic mode, they usually have been relegated quite literally to the margins" (1993b, 115). Jordan's personal narrative, as well as those of Trinh T. Minh-ha, Angela Davis, and Alice Walker take center stage in Parmar's film, offering testimony to the personal and public struggle for ownership of space. June Jordan, for example, remembers a time when she did not feel safe traveling in America, because of the limitations that racism placed upon her body. "I can't do what I want to do with my own body," she states several times in her poetry, adding, "and who in the hell set things up like this?"

A Place of Rage is a heteroglossic participatory documentary that challenges silences. As Janice R. Welsch argues, women's documentaries often include multiple dialogic exchanges in order to "foster dialogue by exposing and challenging the silences created by patriarchy" (170). A heteroglossic approach is consistently found in many African-American women's films and writings. The reciprocity of gazes and verbal exchanges is a hallmark of "participatory art" as defined by Gloria Gibson:

> participatory art sugg[ests] a paradigm for personal and collective introspection and activism. . . . Films by Black independent filmmakers frequently isolate the necessary personal skills needed to interpret and confront issues in everyday life with the hope that a heightened sense of self will lead to individual and collective empowerment. (377)

In *A Place of Rage*, Black lesbian poet June Jordan voices the suppressed rage of African-Americans through her testimony and astute analysis of today's current drug plague within urban African-American neighborhoods. African-Americans have few outlets for rage; indeed, Jordan argues that "rage has lost its respectability since the nineteen sixties." The suppression of rage is matched by a suppression of language, and as Jordan concludes, "When you don't rage, you turn against yourself," leading to apathy, drug use, and collective suicide.

Jordan, Davis, Walker, Minh-ha, and Parmar herself offer exemplifications of women of color who are not afraid to speak their rage who reach out to a young audience and offer them a voice in a participatory dialogue. Even viewers who perceive the world as a dominating hegemony, a world whose language seems alien and incontestable, come to recognize and take part in what linguist Mikhail Bakhtin identifies as "heteroglossia." Bakhtin defines heteroglossia as that which is "aimed sharply and polemically against the official language" (273). Heteroglossia (multitonguedness) guarantees that hegemonic language is always dialogized by "centrifugal" forces, such as that of the voice of June Jordan. Jordan's centrifugal utterances disrupt "centripetal" utterances that, according to Bakhtin, work toward "the victory of one reigning language over the others, the supplanting of languages, their enslavement, the process of illuminating them with the True Word . . . a unitary language of culture and truth . . . and the power of the category of a unitary language" (271).

The speech acts of *A Place of Rage* supplant the hegemonic forces that have relied on the suppression of the voices of African-American women in the history of the Civil Rights movement. American history has been distorted and reframed by an oppressive monologic recounting of African-American history. Alice Walker, June Jordan, and Angela Davis engage in a critique of centripetally informed accounts that suppress the knowledge of the achievements of African women such as Septima Clark, who, Walker reminds us, without the support of a larger Civil Rights movement herself, started schools to teach African-Americans how to read and write so that they could someday vote. Walker stresses the importance of learning about such women who disrupted racist oppression even before African-Americans were able to envision a large Black community as an activist base. Angela Davis speaks about the suppression of knowledge about women's role in the Black Panther movement, and June Jordan speaks about African-American women such as Fannie Lou Hamer, a somewhat forgotten individual who led voter registration efforts in Mississippi, despite daily brutal harassment by the authorities. Jordan is appalled that most people don't remember her and that it took the brutal beating of Hamer in a Mississippi jail at the hands of racist officials to galvanize Americans in the Civil Rights movement. Alice Walker emphasizes the significant achievements of African-American activist women in the churches, women who were "pillars of the movement," though they are often omitted from American history accounts.

Angela Davis calls attention to the importance of language as it attempts

to label her as minority. Davis challenges what Bakhtin describes as "authoritative discourse" (34). Authoritative discourse "strives to determine the very
bases of our ideological interrelations with the world, the very bases of our
behavior. . . . It is so to speak, the word of the fathers" (Bakhtin 342). With her
heteroglossic speech, Angela Davis reclaims her own identity through language
when she states in the film, "We are often called a minority within a minority.
I don't consider myself a minority within a minority. As a matter of fact, I
consider myself a part of a majority within a majority."

Davis' words represent an activist supplanting of authoritative discourse
with what Bakhtin terms "internally persuasive discourse" (342). Using internally persuasive language, Davis comes into a self-actualization, and her performance urges the viewer to rethink the politics of identity, especially the language with which we describe ourselves. Identity is not only dependent upon
self-described subjectivity but also on ownership of space and mobility. Without freedom of movement, whether in language or society, African-American
lesbians and all women are subject to authoritative discourse and oppressive
centripetal forces. Pratibha Parmar brilliantly unites the issues of space ownership and self-ownership by underscoring Davis' words with images of her
jogging and spending time outdoors with her family. Davis speaks about the
need for a collective identity of "women of color," one that is "neither divisive
nor separatist. We do have the right to define an autonomous space for ourselves as women of color when it is necessary. We do have that right." Redefining subjectivity includes "the ongoing reappropriation by women of our
identity, our sexuality, [and] our intellectual power" (Braidotti 256). Physical
mobility, as it is performed through Davis' body, is also an important factor in
subjectivity-making, for "mobility is one of the aspects of freedom, and . . .
the physical dimension is only one aspect; mobility also refers to the intellectual
space of creativity" (Braidotti 256). A Place of Rage celebrates heteroglossia in
what Pascal Bonitzer terms the "free confrontation" (320). A free confrontational cinema is political by virtue of the fact that it is participatory. Rather
than operating in the language of authoritative discourse, it encourages the
viewer to act upon the material or as Pascal Bonitzer would have it, "The free
confrontation is that of contradictory images and witnesses, a mise-en-scène
of the multiple 'facets' of an event by means of interviews and archival documentary footage" (320).

Confronted with a dazzling array of images, the viewer begins to reread in-
terweaved archival footage through a myriad of transgressive heteroglossia,

that of the multiple lesbian African-American narrators. The archival television footage, for example, of Angela Davis as she was interviewed in prison demonstrates how the cameramen and reporter of the original television news program constructed her as if she were a wild animal, interviewed through bulletproof, soundproof glass. Reviewed through Parmar's film, this disturbing television news footage can be deconstructed as a demonizing, colonializing spectacle and a backlash against the Civil Rights movement. Parmar includes the original soundtrack in which a British newsperson speaks of Davis in the unmistakable voice that is used in colonialist documentaries about African people, the voice that constructs the Black woman as an exotic, dangerous threat. Thus *A Place of Rage* calls into question those stereotypical images and values that television viewers tend to correlate with the image of Angela Davis, the Black Panthers, and Black activism in the United States. The mise-en-scène is underscored with Janet Jackson's "Revolution," bringing the confrontational gaze into a rereading of the past, through old grainy stock footage into the present political arena. Rather than constructing the Civil Rights movement as something finished in the past, Parmar represents it as an active presence in American society, freeing it from a visual history that has constructed it as a finished event.

A Place of Rage's visual spectacles and speech acts draw allegiances between the Civil Rights movement and the Gay/Lesbian/Bisexual/Transsexual activist movement. Alice Walker, for example, comments that the lesbian characters included in her novels often provoke anger within her readership. Walker sees this as a backlash against both people of color and lesbians, gays and bisexuals. Similarly, Angela Davis and June Jordan testify to the direct link between violence against gay/lesbian/bisexual people and racist attacks. Pratibha Parmar's authorial presence as Black South Asian lesbian infuses the film with a postmodern subjectivity, one that Susan Rubin Suleiman supports, to "forge the bonds of community by 'smaller and more local' links, and by 'imaginative identification with the details of others' lives' " (232). By the same token, Parmar invites the viewer to forge such bonds with their own post-modern subjectivities, reaching across the trajectory of the cinematic apparatus to engage in an active heteroglossic dialogue with the image-making, history-making process. Appropriately enough, the film ends with a song that invites the viewer into the participatory act of struggle: "If you're ready, come go with me," sing the Staple Singers, voicing Pratibha Parmar and all the individuals of the Civil Rights movement.

Pratibha Parmar's *Warrior Marks* (1993) is perhaps her most remarkable performative documentary to date. Alice Walker produced the film and also appears in it. Walker's novel, *Possessing the Secret of Joy*, which deals with female genital mutilation, was an inspiration for *Warrior Marks*. Female genital mutilation affects over one hundred million women in the world. Pratibha Parmar and Alice Walker interviewed women from Senegal, Gambia, Burkino Faso, and England who are either concerned with or who actually experienced female genital mutilation. The interviews are intercut with Alice Walker's views on the subject and a performative tableau of an African-American woman, "Richelle," dancing an interpretive performance. The most astounding footage, however, is the interviews with women who actually perform the ritual act of female genital mutilation. Their inability and refusal to question such a thoroughly misogynist tradition angers Walker, Parmar, and the viewer. Parmar is careful to exhibit the cultural context of the practice, but, as Walker asks, if it were a cultural practice to murder women, would we sanction such an act as a cultural ritual? Parmar and Walker insist that all women rethink racist and misogynist "cultural practices" that brutalize women on a daily basis.

In Alice Walker and Pratibha Parmar's book on the making of *Warrior Marks*, Parmar discusses the critical reception of the film. Parmar has been confronted with questions related to cultural imperialism, essentialism, and the taboo against Western intervention against female genital mutilation. Parmar responds:

> The fear of being labeled cultural imperialists and racists has made many women reluctant to say or do anything about female genital mutilation. Except for the writings and voices of a handful of white feminists over the last decade or so, there has been a deafening silence . . . this reluctance to interfere with other cultures leaves African children at risk of mutilation. (Walker and Parmar 94–95)

In *Warrior Marks*, Parmar manages to negotiate a transitional space to elicit justice. Her strategic deconstruction of binaries between "first" and "third" world knowledge works against normalizing, essentializing projects that promote silence around the issue of female genital mutilation. As Jane Flax writes, "One aspect of these deconstructive projects is to loosen the hold of transcendental or rationalistic theories of subjectivity and justice" (114). Flax continues, "Justice teaches us how to reconcile or tolerate differences between subjects and others without domination" (123). *Warrior Marks* seeks justice and change while at the same time it recognizes cultural differences. Parmar's sensitivity to the problematics of representation across cultural borders is balanced by her bravery and self-reflectivity. She asks herself:

> How can I create a sensitive and respectful representation of people—and a continent—who have historically been grossly misrepresented? How can *Warrior Marks* begin to challenge the cultural imperialist imagery of Africa and Africans, as perpetuated in Hollywood films like *Out of Africa*? (Walker and Parmar 95)

Determined not to present female genital mutilation as culturally sanctioned by Third World practice, Parmar sees it as an act of violence against women. For example, as she reminds us, all over the world women undergo physical mutilations that are "equally devastating" (Walker and Parmar 109), such as anorexia/bulimia, breast implants, and so forth. Parmar walks as a woman along the borders of identity and subjectivity and opens up a filmic site of transnational feminist practice. As Caren Kaplan reminds us, "We need critical practices that mediate . . . interrogating the terms that mythologize our differences and similarities" (138). By using extensive filmed testimonies, Parmar negotiates a multiple "female subaltern subject constructed within a heterogeneous and disruptive contextualization" (Carr 157). The testimonies are intercut with a dance sequence that is open to interpretation.

Parmar hoped that "dance would evoke the symbolic resonance of this story, as opposed to being illustrative" (Walker and Parmar 222). A dancer, "Richelle," performs in front of a rear-projection of filmed testimony of Gambian girls waiting to be circumcised and mutilated. The viewer is faced with a collaborative interweaving of both realism and staged theatrics that are open to interpretation. The dance sequence fosters a sense of agency/urgency in the viewer, who is bodily inscribed in an interpretive space "where descriptions and readings are negotiated and renegotiated" (Walker and Parmar 229). Such a space is described by Lorraine Code as a space of debate, or as dance theorist Judith Lynne Hanna explains:

> The significance of a dance performance and its context can be reinvented through talking and writing about it . . . after the performance, when the dance remains etched in memory, the replay of the dancing surges forth in our thought to evoke the fire in a new transformation. (198)

Parmar's inclusion of the performative dance is an innovative and decidedly corporeal way to communicate ideas, promote humanity, and foster debate.

Parmar herself came to this realization, as she began intercutting the dance sequences with the testimony of mutilation, "it dawned on me how much this film is about bodies and body language, a celebration of women's bodies despite their mutilation" (Walker and Parmar 225). Parmar's authorial voice enacts a dialogic, one that both interrogates the marking/mutilation/subjection of female bodies and at the same time explores the sensuality/beauty of women's bodies.

The performative aspects of *Warrior Marks* produce anger as much as healing. In a sense, *Warrior Marks* operates in the discourse of what performance theorist Richard Schechner calls, "phatic theatre" (1988, 216), in which performance promotes healing, wherein "a balance is struck among the public, the private, and the secret" (1988, 231). Far from being static locations of taboo knowledge, Parmar's phatic performative reminds us that performances change participants. Parmar's phatic dialogic, between healing and waking the spectator enacts a principle of performative consciousness: "The beauty of 'performance consciousness' is that it activates alternatives . . . performance consciousness is subjective, full of alternatives and potentiality" (Schechner 1985, 6). Too often critics reduce filmic performativity, especially danced performative bodies, to static, objectified spectacle, however, in *Warrior Marks* we are reminded of the multivalent and endlessly irreducible sites of meaning of the performing body in cinematic spectacle. Marco De Marinis, an Italian semiotician, remarks:

> Action and *the simulation of action* combine and corroborate each other . . . performance always provokes *effects of the real* as well as *theatrical effects* . . . in the sense of its real production of meanings, kinds of awareness, events, and lived experiences. (157)

Warrior Marks brings us into the simulacrum of the lived experience of genital mutilation through dance rather than graphic visuals of the actual practice. Such visuals have, in other documentaries on this subject, tended to emphasize the distance between the viewer and the subject, denying any sense of collective agency, or collective urgency, much less any sense of diasporic female community. Embodiment in *Warrior Marks* traverses the duality of subject-object relationships seen in most colonialist documentary cinema. The gaze of the performative dancer invites us into her psychological, phenomenological, and corporeal experience, enacting "lived-body theory" (13) as defined by dance theorist Sondra Horton Fraleigh, who writes that lived-body ideals " hold that the body is *lived* as a body-of-action. Human movement is the actualization, the realization, of embodiment. . . . Embodiment is not passive, it is articulate" (13).

The spectacle of the particular dance sequence in *Warrior Marks* in which Richelle relives genital mutilation, writhing in pain and agony, demands participatory identification. Herbert Blau describes this aspect of performance as "an insistence upon meaning" (96). In terms of South Asian thought, the viewer enters a zone beyond subject/object binaries. As Phillip B. Zarrilli argues, within Indian culture, such a phenomenon is known as "tat tvam asi" (you are that). " 'You are that' asserts a fundamental identity between microcosm and macrocosm, the individual self and the universe; a person can become one-with and join-with; there is no object set over against a subject" (Zarrilli, 145).

The combination of testimony with dance performance in *Warrior Marks* deprivileges the veil of difference in a performative gesture of graphic, yet phatic politics. As spectator, "tat tvam asi" you are that, you cannot help but become at least to some degree at one with women and girls who are subject to the practice of female genital mutilation. You are moved to action and moved toward the possibility of healing and the regaining of lost female sexuality. Alice Walker writes, in the introduction of *Warrior Marks*:

> When I saw the completed *Warrior Marks*, I recognized it as a symbol of our mutual daring and trust. It is a powerful and magnificent film, thanks to Pratibha's brilliance as director, constructed from our grief and anger and pain. But also from our belief in each other, our love of life, our gratitude that we are women of color able to offer our sisters a worthy gift after so many centuries of tawdriness, and our awareness of those other "companion spirits" we know are out there. (Walker and Parmar 4)

The films of Pratibha Parmar critique anthropological and white feminists construction of an "Other." They make us review the politics of appropriation and colonization. They resituate who speaks and who listens. Parmar's oeuvre is an oppositionally coded participatory cinema of activism. Her films challenge identity politics and alterity itself. Her performative, heteroglossic, celebratory, confrontational, multivoiced, corporeal, interrogating gaze is informed by her own authorial presence as a woman of Kenya and South Asia, a lesbian of the diaspora. In the words of Alice Walker in a poem for Pratibha Parmar published in *Warrior Marks*, "As we work/together/we begin/to rebuild/the/shattered/ancient/foundation/of/the/universal/family/of/women" (Walker and Parmar 59). The African and Asian diasporic vision of Pratibha Parmar begins such a project.

❖ 6 ❖

TRINH T. MINH-HA
"An empowering notion of difference"

BORN IN VIETNAM in 1953, Trinh T. Minh-ha came to the United States, studied music and comparative literature at the University of Illinois, and she studied ethnomusicology in France. Her later experience as a researcher in Senegal led directly to her first film work, *Reassemblage* (1982), a poetic transgressive film that transcends and revolutionizes cinema. Trinh T. Minh-ha's films are extraordinary examples of *l'écriture feminine* that combine her unique talents as writer, composer, filmmaker, and theorist.

The most exciting and, at the same time unnerving, distinguishing element of the oeuvre of Trinh T. Minh-ha is an uncanny mastery of those hybrid spaces or borders between categories: between fiction and nonfiction, art and autobiography, between documentary and document, between subject and object, viewer and viewed and identity as subscribed, and identity as self-inscribed. In an interview with Judith Mayne, reprinted in *Framer Framed* (1992), Mayne and Trinh T. Minh-ha discuss borderlines; in particular the borderlines that are routinely subscribed or inscribed on the body of the "Third World" artist. As a writer, Trinh T. Minh-ha found that her nondiscursive text, *Woman, Native, Other,* was initially met with resistance from many publishers. Eager to "eat the other," in the words of bell hooks, publishers were frankly interested in Trinh as an artist "from the Third World." Nevertheless her text was initially rejected. As Trinh put it, "attempts at introducing a break into the fixed norms of the master's confidant prevailing discourses are easily misread, dismissed, or obscured in the name of 'good writing,' of 'theory,' or of 'scholarly work.' " (Minh-ha 1992, 138).

The space of the borderline, the taboo, the untranslatable, is the intersubjective space of Trinh's writing and films. The struggle to mark new space, reframe boundaries is one that women writers and filmmakers of color are remapping in a struggle to conjure and write the body in a way that is actively "articulating this always emerging-already-distorted place that remains so difficult, on the one hand, for the First World to even recognize, and on the other, for our own communities to accept" (Minh-ha 1992, 139).

In an effort to transform cinema into a means of "speaking nearby" her "subjects" (African women in *Reassemblage,* and *Naked Spaces—Living Is Round* [1985], Vietnamese women in *Surname Viet Given Name Nam* [1989], and Chinese women in *Shoot for the Contents* [1991]), Trinh T. Minh-ha re- structures the postcolonial gaze and its manufacturing device that almost guar- antees a limited subject/object relationship between viewer and viewed. Trinh's films have often been critically received (and reduced) as antiethnographies, antidocumentaries, and other reductionist categories. Ironically, the voice-over in *Reassemblage* criticizes "the habit of imposing a meaning to every single sign," as if playfully to outwit the viewer's attempts to reduce the film to a limited Euroidentified category.

Reassemblage embarks on a radical, ludic deconstruction of documentary form and ethnographic film practice (especially in its avoidance of the reduc- tion of Third World "subjects" into flattened out figures of sublimated desire and lack) in terms of subjectivity, alterity, and identity. Most certainly *Reas- semblage* speaks nearby documentary gesturing toward its colonialist objecti- fication of African women. However, the critique of documentary and ethnog- raphy are only some examples of border crossings in *Reassemblage.* It would be reductionist for me to attempt to identify the "subjects" of this film. I can only speak nearby some of them, feeling all too aware of my habit of "imposing a meaning to every sign." I can only say that, as a filmmaker and performance artist, I'm highly aware of the highly performative quality of the film's struc- ture, with its use of abrupt jump cuts, black leader, silence on the track, non- eyematches, bursts of repetitive voice-overs and disarming close-ups of the faces and bodies of African women. These experimental techniques are remi- niscent of those used by New Wave filmmakers such as Jean-Luc Godard and experimental women filmmakers, such as Maya Deren. *Reassemblage* is self-re- flective in its voicing of self-questioning. "A film about what? My friends ask." Trinh, in the voice-over, interrupts, much in the manner of any number of self- reflective comments found in Jean-Luc Godard's films. This Godardian mo- ment announces that *Reassemblage* is not so much a documentary as a docu- ment, a poetic essay-film that speaks nearby its subject: Senegalese women.

In *The Woman at the Keyhole,* Judith Mayne finds that Trinh T. Minh-ha "questions the very possibility of seizing the reality of Senegal through such a visual documentation" (212). Trinh's voice-over deconstructs traditions of the colonialist documentary, critiquing Western notions of a unified "Third World feminine" alterity. The visual barrage of African female breasts refigures the Black female body as a marker in the discourse of ethnographic practice, medical discourse, and the clinical gaze. As if literally to remap the icon of the female breast, which conjures the Westerner's routine signification of breast as fetishized object, Trinh uses repetition to reframe this image beyond the borders of Western voyeuristic film spectatorship.

While we gaze at the breasts of Senegalese women, the image gazes at us and the soundtrack disarms our critically reductionist impulses. This is a performative gesture that works on the viewer in a gesture of endlessly signifying self-reflexivity. On the soundtrack, for example, we hear an African tale that underscores African women's subjective space in oral storytelling tradition, thus recontextualizing the breast as signifier on and in non-Western terms. Through the story of woman (depicted as fire) we learn of the signifier of woman as the possessor of fire, that which destroys and at the same time regenerates. The voice-over on the soundtrack intones, "Only she knew how to make fire. She kept it in diverse places. At the end of the stick she used to dig the ground with, for example, in her nails or in her fingers."

Thus, the female body becomes a transcendent signifier that rejects those borders defined by medical literature, psychoanalytic literature, and the gaze of the ethnographer and documentarist. Later in *Reassemblage*, the voice-over returns to fire as a perception of women's embodied presence. "The fire place and woman's face. The pot is known as a universal symbol for the Mother, the Grandmother, the Goddess." The breast no longer reveals, perhaps it never did reveal, according to the performative logic of *Reassemblage*: "Nudity does not reveal. The hidden in its absence."

Reassemblage critiques the so-called "mastery" of the documentary film over the ostensible "subject." By relegating the disembodied voice-over to "the eternal commentary that escorts images," Trinh T. Minh-ha moves the borders of objecthood to subjectivity, for in *Reassemblage* the images seem to escort the commentary, in a self-reflective enunciation of unique *l'écriture feminine*. *Reassemblage*, as Judith Mayne points out, "explores the significance of oral traditions," both through the use of the filmmaker and the female voices of Senegalese women themselves (1990, 216). These voices speak in a dissonant, yet poetic unity. Mayne reads this gesture as a rejection of any presumed unity of "Third World subject" and yet "the very division between the voice and the image suggests the possibility of another kind of observation, one resistant to the dualities of 'West' versus 'Third World' " (1990, 216). *Reassemblage* revolutionizes spectatorship by demanding a kinship between the semiotic and symbolic boundaries, which become fluid and thus "demand a new means of perception on the part of its spectators" (Daly 245).

Reassemblage problematizes theoretical consideration as much as it invites active performative spectatorship. Its Kantian perspective moves the viewer into a reactive specular positionality. As Adorno remarks, postmodernist art can show us "something on that other side of reality's veil" (23). Documentarists and ethnographers have sought to unveil the supposedly "primitive Third World Female Other" from the perspective of "mastery." The so-called "objective" documentary perspective has served to intensify the veil, enshrouding the "Other" in layers of the veil. Who is Robert Flaherty's Nanook? Who is Nanook's wife? Who are the "subjects" of African documents, documentarists' texts? If *Reassemblage* undertakes a radical repositioning of ethnographic space, *Naked Spaces* remaps spatial questions into the area of ethnomusicological explorations of sound, voice, and translation.

Trinh's filmmaking exposes the veil that enshrouds the ethnographer. The ideology of the lens as captor is exposed as a myth. The "objective" documentarist has captured nothing more than a mere signifier of his own subjectivity reflected in the eyes of his subject. Trinh T. Minh-ha exposes this irony in an aside in *Reassemblage* in which the ethnographer, the voice-over states, is sleeping next to his switched-on tape recorder missing his opportunity to "capture his subject. " The mimetic capacity of ethnography is a flawed and veiled prospect. "To copy reality reduced reality and the copy becomes a veiled substitute," states the voice-over. My reading of *Reassemblage* celebrates its embrace of self-reflectivity and performative reinscriptions. *Reassemblage* is a film poem, an essay that "speaks nearby" African female subjectivity. The dissonance across images, sound, and signifiers is ludic. Embracing "the determinate and indeterminate [that which] remains ambiguous even after they have been synthesized" (Adorno 181), the active spectator partakes in a border transgression. Writing on the work of Trinh T. Minh-ha is a border transgression in the sense of critic as translator. Aware of my capacity as "translator," even as I attempt to write nearby my subject, I am reminded of Derrida's location of the woman translator as empowering: "the woman translator is not simply subordained, she is not the author's secretary. . . . translation is writing . . . productive writing called forth by the original text" (153).

The complexities of translation is one of the central explorations of *Naked Spaces—Living Is Round* (1985). In particular, the viewer as translator is located at the border of a critical rupturing of Eurocentric notions of the sounds of voices of "foreign" tongues. In particular, Trinh T. Minh-ha emphasizes the sounds of different dialects in several African women's voices (from Senegal, Mauritania, Togo, Haiti, Burkina Faso, and elsewhere). *Naked Spaces* differs from *Reassemblage* in that it is a longer text that contemplates the viewer's need/desire for translation. Three voice-overs are heard in the film that takes as its subject, loosely translated, women's living spaces. Trinh problematizes this work in her use of natural low-light conditions of indoor spaces that are juxtaposed against outdoor spaces lit with harsh available natural light. In an interview entitled "Film as Translation," republished in *Framer Framed*, Laura Mulvey writes that both *Reassemblage* and *Naked Spaces* have soundtracks that are unique in their "movement back and forth between music, other everyday sounds, the various narratives and silences" (Minh-ha 1992, 121). One of the statements contained in the soundtrack of *Naked Spaces* specifically questions Western notions of "proper" music and sounds:

> In certain societies where sounds have become letters with sharps and flats, those unfortunate enough not to fit into these letters are tossed out of the system and qualified unmusical. They are called noises. *It is known that one of the primary tasks of ethnomusicologists is to study what traditional societies consider music and what they reject as non-music.* (Minh-ha 1992, 23)

In the interview with Mulvey, Trinh explains, "I fare with ease in the world of experimental music, perhaps because of the cultural hybridity of both its instrumentation and its deterritorialized space" (Minh-ha 1992, 121). The use of music, sound, and silence to transgress space adds a performative element to *Naked Spaces* and *Reassemblage* that almost transcends the need for any type of translation, despite Western notions of music and sound. Trinh remaps subjectivities across the boundaries of identity by cross-cutting sound (music and voices) of various different African dwellings, breaking a taboo of both ethnography and ethnomusicology. The manipulation of sound ruptures fixed notions of identity, for "the understanding of identification as an enacted fantasy of incorporation . . . that coherence is desired, wished for, idealized" (Butler, 136). *Naked Spaces* denies the translating act of corporeal signification and at the same time critiques the manner in which "the peoples of Third World countries used to be lumped together in an undifferentiated Otherness" (Minh-ha 124).

Naked Spaces marks the integral feature of the universalized Third World Other as it has been mimetically sealed in Western art, or, in the eyes of Adorno, it shows us "the phenomena of the replaced" (257). Working from Kant's writing, Adorno speaks of the phenomenon of how "knowledge of how to produce a phenomenon can replace the experience of what it it" (257). Thus instead of a film of "commentary that escorts images," as Trinh describes traditional ethnography, *Naked Spaces* reverses the spectatorial identifactory process. As Mulvey sees it, "The imagery is kind of a grid which the spectator can consider your [Trinh's] manipulations of sound" (125). Trinh elaborates on the point, "the choice here was to have that transgressive fluidity in the sound" (125). Minh-ha uses a similarly performative montage of disjunctive sounds and images in *Reassemblage*.

Rhetorically, *Naked Spaces* conflates a number of theoretical attempts to reconstitute "woman's space"—for example, Laura Mulvey's "ludic" space, Teresa de Lauretis' notion of off-screen space, Julia Kristeva's notion of the prelinguistic space of the chora, or Luce Irigaray's rereading of psychoanalytic "lack" of a voicing of the female body. Indeed, *Naked Spaces* conjures Cixous' writing of the body across a grid of space junctures in a constant flux. At the same time, the film opens up an entirely new configuration of space as "women's space," inviting the viewer into this performative evocation. Trinh T. Minh-ha's border crossings freely appropriate new and taboo areas of space; not only for women, but for multiple subject formations. *Naked Spaces* locates a textual space making, a clearing and entering, a constant shifting of subjective identities and signifiers. Knowledge, women's knowledge, is discursive and dialogic; it is ruptured and resignified as mobile and fluctuating. *Naked Spaces* moves the borders of narrative filmmaking itself between those walls of ethnography, personal film, experimental film, and documentary. Not unsurprisingly, the critical reception to *Naked Spaces* and *Reassemblage* was problematic, according to Trinh T. Minh-ha. Many viewers were unprepared for the formal elements of the films. Those who were willing to undergo the formalism of *Reassemblage* had little patience for the extreme long takes of *Naked Spaces*. The politics and poetic transgressions of *Reassemblage* are in some ways less difficult to translate or discern than those of *Naked Spaces*.

Interestingly enough, Trinh comments that Native-American viewers in particular responded to *Naked Spaces* with "intense and exalted feedback" (Minh-ha 1992, 131). The habitation of space, particularly "women's" space and "Third World" space, is a critical hobby-horse of late, but *Naked Spaces* constructs and deconstructs space in a anti-Cartesian manner perhaps more in keeping with Native-American and African-American conceptions of community, space, and storytelling. The "subjects" of *Naked Spaces* are essentially whole different living spaces, spaces that remain on-screen for seemingly lengthy sections of film. *Naked Spaces* conjures the specular pleasures of images of spaces of mobility rendered in the context of the long-take in both *Re-assemblage* and *Naked Spaces*. African women look at the viewer for lengthy periods of time. Is this look "contained" within the borders of the frame? Marc Vernet writes, "the look of the camera has a double effect; it foregrounds the enunciative distance of the filmic text and attacks the spectator's voyeurism by putting the space of the film and the space of the movie theater briefly in direct contact" (48).

As a viewer, one experiences these looks, not as looks at the camera, but as direct gazes at ourselves as viewers. The films of Trinh T. Minh-ha are thus examples of post-story films as defined by Mas'ud Zavarzadeh: "a post-story film . . . [which is] a post-modern political meditation on the cultural discontinuities of late capitalism and the place of woman in it" (as qtd. in Dixon 42). *Naked Spaces* as post-story film rearticulates notions of film space and filmic pleasure across the specular regime of spectatorship and sound reception. It seeks new ground and asks questions such as those posed by Michel de Certeau: "how does time articulate itself on an organized space? How does it effect its 'break-through' in the occasional mode? In short, what constitutes the implantation of memory in a place . . . ?" (86).

Poststructuralist notions of women's space go hand in hand with a search for a definition of knowledge as it is created by on-screen women subjects and off-screen sounds in *Naked Spaces*. Trinh T. Minh-ha locates the space sought after by Lyotard; where the difference between conversational knowledge and ordinary spoken discourse partakes in a dialogic exchange, where, "the interlocutors use any available ammunition, changing games from one utterance to the next: questions, requests, assertions, and narratives are launched pell mell into battle. . . . The rules allow and encourage the greatest possible flexibility of utterance" (17). The implicit rules of traditional filmmaking have denied any sort of physical or philosophical interaction between participants on and off-screen, and the filmmaker herself. Trinh T. Minh-ha moves toward a performative feminist dialogic through this extraordinary and often unexpected use of countermoves.

Surname Viet Given Name Nam (1989), Trinh T. Minh-ha's next film, crosses the boundaries of "acceptable" or "appropriate" ethnographic filmmaking in the inclusion of restaged interviews of five Vietnamese women. The "staged" qualities of the interviews disrupt the received notions of veracity in documentary technique. Instead of "collecting" interviews on film of "subjects" (as objects), Minh-ha decided to overturn the idea of "objective" recording of talking heads by deliberately and carefully choosing interviews and actors to reperform these "interviews." Five women were chosen and then asked to help define themselves by their choices in clothing and camera work, lighting and gesture. In short, they became "actors," acting "themselves," thus calling into question the veracity of "non-staged" interviews in traditional documentary filmmaking.

As Trinh T. Minh-ha told Laura Mulvey, the strategy of restaging interviews initially provoked strong reactions; some positive and some negative, "some viewers were furious because they expected to be told about it at the outset of the film" (Minh-ha 1992, 146). Truth and its construction are scrutinized by this blatant overturning of the "rules" of documentary filmmaking. As the filmmaker comments, "by playing with the false and the true at work in the two kinds of truth, what is taken for granted in interviews suddenly becomes very prominent" (Minh-ha 1992, 146). The boundaries of "fiction" and "non-fiction" are re/located at the nexus of a dialectic that forces the viewer into a discourse on the question of "who is speaking." This is further represented in the film by the use of a combination of extradiegetic text scrawling across the screen with voice-overs, and diegetic speech in both Vietnamese and English, sometimes translated and subtitled, and sometimes left deliberately "untranslated."

Text, speech, "Otherness," and the identity of "Third World Women" are scrutinized and problematized by the performative formalistic strategies in *Surname Viet Given Name Nam*. Speech utterances, text that is translated into performance, the spoken words orchestrate themselves in a manner that defies hermeneutics. This departure from hermeneutical taxonomy is repeatedly underscored in the film with statements of self-reflexivity such as "Spoken, transcribed and translated. From listening to recording; speech to writing. You can talk, we can cut, trim, tidy up."

Often, as above, Trinh directly confronts her own formal practice, as in the statement, "By choosing the most direct and spontaneous form of voicing and documentary, I find myself closer to fiction" (Minh-ha 1992, 78). The viewer is drawn into a performed heteroglossalis, one in which one must choose whether to listen or to read the text, whether to look for "truth," or respond to fiction. The voice-over also poses the question, "Do you translate by eye or ear?" Suddenly the term "translation" is rife with multiplying signifiers. Viewership becomes an act of translation; filmmaking is translation of fictions into truths and truths into fictions. Identity is also a form of translation, a translation from the subject to object, from who one is to who one is perceived to be. Speech itself is a translation of self, identity, and its markers. Who is the Vietnamese woman speaking? Who is the Third World subject? Just as the film itself is untranslatable (and at the same time endlessly signifying), the subject-object relationship itself is unknowable, yet it registers itself through a subjectivity usually not present in dominant cinema. The subject as text is self-translating.

Watching a screen is an act of translation, and, as Minh-ha reminds us in the voice-over, "Translation seeks faithfulness and accuracy and ends up always betraying either the letter of the text, its spirit, or its aesthetics . . . grafting several languages, cultures and realities onto a single body. The problem of translation, after all, is a problem of reading and identity." *Surname Viet Given Name Nam* demonstrates the importance of the unspoken politics of translation, while carefully transcending the borders of erasure, denial of difference, and conflation of identity.

Trinh T. Minh-ha moves in a discourse of female authorship which recovers the objectified Other's discourse, upping the ante on Gayatri Spivak's question, "Can the Subaltern Speak?" Speaking subjects in this film (Tran Thi Hien, Khien Lai, Ngo Kim Nhuy, and Tran Thi Bich Yen) turn persuasive discourse into speaking persons, "fictions" into "truths" in a struggle which Bakhtin describes as creative and self-liberating:

> This process becomes especially important in those cases where a subject is striving to liberate [her]self from the influence of such an image and its discourse by means of objectification, or in striving to expose the limitations of both image and discourse. . . . All this creates fertile soil for objectifying another's discourse. (348)

As spectators, particularly Western spectators, we are scrutinized by the on-screen participants. Our discourse of film pleasure is deconstructed in and by our viewership: we are faced with the gazes and voices of a panoply of resistant storytellers who preclude our preconceptions and epistemologies of solid ground. Ngo Kim Nhuy, as "Kim," for example, voices her resistance to objectification: "At first I was very hesitant when you asked me to participate, but then I thought: why would I refuse, when I am a Vietnamese woman myself, and the role in the film speaks the truth of the Vietnamese women still in Vietnam as well as those emigrated to the U.S.?" This resistant gesture of anti-compliance is an exemplification of one that often "occurs [when there is] a separation between internally persuasive discourse and authoritarian enforced discourse" (Bakhtin, 345). Discourse is questioned, the "Third World subject" becomes an individualized subject, and her enunciation exposes the boundaries of Western subject-object relations.

Surname Viet Given Name Nam has provoked hostility, according to

Minh-ha. In fact, it provokes so many varying reactions in viewers. Because of the overt feminist politics of the staged interviews, many viewers, the film-maker tells Laura Mulvey, show a "lack of concern . . . for any earnest inquiry into gender politics" (Minh-ha 1992, 132). Others are uncomfortable with the lack of a binaristic model of North/South, or communist/anti-communist system in the film:

> These viewers tend to deny or worse, to *obscure* entirely the question of gender by constantly casting the Vietnam reality back into the binary. . . . They also seem to be more preoccupied with what they militated for, or more eager to preserve an idealized image of Vietnam they supported, than they are willing to look at the actual situation of post-revolutionary Vietnam. (Minh-ha 1992, 132)

Surname Viet Given Name Nam enacts the discourse of "female identity closure," which Trinh T. Minh-ha alludes to in her book *Woman, Native, Other.* The "Third World woman subject" (a category which I am only using for the purpose of arguing against its presupposition as available label) is, at least in some discourse practices, a category that suppresses the postcolonial feminist speaker. As Trinh T. Minh-ha writes, "the difference (within) between *difference* itself and *identity* has so often been ignored and the use of the two terms so readily confused, that claiming a female/ethnic identity/difference is commonly tantamount to reviving a kind of naive 'male tinted' romanticism" (Minh-ha 1989, 96). Thus, the films of Trinh T. Minh-ha threaten to disrupt the definitions of "Third World," "feminist," and an essentialist definition of a "Non-Western woman." Remaking language, resubjectifying identity, and unmasking veils of difference are postcolonial moves away from authoritative discourse toward internally persuasive gestures. The writing and filmmaking of Trinh T. Minh-ha refutes reductive readings of the very concept of "Third World," and "woman," and a host of other homogenizing, globalizing terms. What is a "Vietnamese woman" after a screening of *Surname Viet Given Name Nam*? How do we define African women after seeing *Reassemblage* and *Naked Spaces—Living Is Round*? How do we construct identity? Minh-ha argues that identity has its uses, though she underscores the importance of resistance:

> Again, if it is a point of redeparture for those of us whose ethnicity and gender were historically debased, then identity remains necessary as a political/personal strategy of survival and resistance. But if it is essentialized as an end point, a point of "authentic" arrival, then it only narrows the struggle. (Minh-ha 1992, 157)

Trinh T. Minh-ha politicizes issues of identity and difference. Her films invoke a multiply formed, constantly moving, negotiating identity. This mobile deconstruction and reconstruction of identity repoliticizes difference issues in ways that inform the multiply produced subjectivities. With *Shoot for the Contents* (1991), Trinh T. Minh-ha moved her cinematic gaze to China and Chinese women. Once again, Minh-ha crosses the borders of insider/outsider status, as she does in her films on Africa. In an interview with Nancy N. Chen, "Speaking Nearby," Trinh T. Minh-ha explains that she feels free to traverse cultural borders, "instead of minding our own business as we have been herded to" (435). Once again Minh-ha forces a rereading of borders of identity (in this case the parameters of the "Third World" filmmaker). "Having one's work explained (or brought to closure) through one's personality," she quips, "is the best way to escape the issues of power, knowledge, and subjectivity raised" (Chen 436). She approached the subject of feminism and China from the point of view of "speaking nearby," a mode that she tells Chen "does not objectify, does not point to an object as if it is distant from the speaking subject or absent from the speaking place" (443).

It wouldn't be going too far from the idea of speaking nearby to suggest that in *Shoot for the Contents*, the camera gazes near its multiple subjects: language, women, the body, Mao, writing, and the camera apparatus itself. Nor would I be straying too far, I think, from Trinh's statement if I said that the soundtrack of *Shoot for the Contents* invites the listener to hear nearby. The voice-overs and speakers do less guiding of the listener than gesturing. The camera lingers on objects, a street scene, for example, jumping to a close-up of a young Chinese girl. The structure, says the filmmaker, "is devised precisely so as to emphasize the heterogeneity of Chinese society and the profound differences within it" (Chen 446). However, *Shoot for the Contents* cannot be neatly assigned to the category of the film poem.

Shoot for the Contents, Trinh T. Minh-ha states, is neither "illogical, elliptical, and metaphorical" nor "logical, linear, and dogmatic" (Chen 446). It is both poetic and political, in terms of language and cinematic device. The visuals are lyrical and poetic, bathed in light, classically framed—beautifully photographed calligraphy for example. The speakers are both Chinese and "non-Native." For example, an African scholar speaks at length on China and its colonialist history. The teachings of Mao and Confucius are appropriated and at times conflated. "Such a merging is both amusing and extremely ironic for those of us who are familiar with Chinese history" (Chen 448). What is probably the most fascinating and compelling feature of *Shoot for the Contents*, and for the films of Trinh T. Minh-ha, is their endless movement between fixed and unfixed signifiers, or, as the filmmaker herself calls it, "the 'unsutured' process of meaning production" (Chen 450). Trinh T. Minh-ha moves the burden of struggle, the (delightful yet frustrating) work of the mind, from the subject to the viewer. The viewer is thrust into the position of knowing his or her own positionality.

Trinh T. Minh-ha's most recent film, *A Tale of Love*, co-directed with Jean-Paul Bourdier, is an experimental film that follows the narrative of Kieu, a freelance Vietnamese-American writer who supports herself as a sex worker/model. The film is constructed around Kieu's growing self-awareness as she investigates and writes on the Vietnamese nineteenth-century poem "The Tale of Kieu." Kieu and Trinh T. Minh-ha renarrate the poem in a performative feminist postcolonial act of resignification. Kieu acts as a transgressive figure who guides herself (and the viewer) through a postmodern rendering of "The Tale of Love" as she lifts the veil from the voyeuristic act of spectatorship and narrative. The narrative itself deconstructs and reconstructs narrative into a scopic regime of fluidity between the borders of memory, reality, and fantasy.

"The Tale of Love," the poem on which the film is based, is the Vietnamese poem of love, and it is comparable to the love story of Romeo and Juliet. In the poem, a martyred woman sacrifices her "purity" and prostitutes herself for the good of her family. As Kieu states in the film, "Kieu" is a powerful allegorical figure for Vietnamese of the diaspora: "Kieu is a folk symbol of love. She is both passionately admired and blamed." "Kieu" has come to represent Vietnam herself. Kieu unravels and unpacks the poem as she researches and writes about the poem. In between her meditations on the meaning of the poem, Kieu supports her free-lance writing by posing for a photographer, Alikan, who shrouds her body in veils and won't allow her to look at him while he looks at her.

Kieu frustrates her traditional family members by her pursuit of a career as a writer, rather than her pursuit of a "suitable" marriage. She is in love with writing. She finds pleasure in dreaming and fantasy, in living the poem she seeks to understand. After her aunt reminds her of the saying that "She who has no husband is like a bed with no nails," she explains that she needs a room of her own to write, for "It is writing that I am in love with." Female creativity is closely linked with Kieu's quest for knowledge as is rehearsed as a passionate and erotic, pleasurable sense of knowledge and imagination. Kieu's quest exposes how in fact "romantic love is an imaginary dimension of the poetic power of the imagination" as Monika Treut reminds us (118). As the film unfolds, and Kieu begins to write more and more frequently, the film becomes less and less linear, and we are treated to elliptic fantasy sequences from the subjective point of view of Kieu. As in romantic love literature, which combines fantasies of pleasure and pain, Kieu exists in a liminal state of desire. Kieu's foremost desire is to rework desires that objectify her into fantasies that deny Alikan (and the viewer) the voyeuristic pleasures that are designed around the eroticism of headless female bodies. In a key scene, Kieu goes to Alikan's studio and watches him watching another model who is told not to look at the photographer, and to keep her head covered.

"You don't want a nude," she tells him, "what you want is a female body without a head." Here Trinh T. Minh-ha exposes the link between sexual voyeurism and the virtual decapitation of women in love stories, at the same time involving Kieu as a quest-heroine who looks without-being-looked-at, a role usually carried out by the photographer, filmmaker, and spectator-as-voyeur. Kieu ponders voyeurism in the context of "The Tale of Kieu" and undergoes a process of self-recreation that moves beyond the divided nature of knowledge of the self and knowledge of the erotic female body. Her self-knowledge goes against the grain of Western Kantian binarisms that split eroticism from rational philosophical inquiry, suppressing women and Eros in a quest for rational thought. As philosopher Robin May Schott explains, "Kant's hostility toward sensuality is correlated with a dismissal of women as sexual beings who are incapable of thought" (129). A Tale of Love reimagines and regrounds the erotic within the boundaries of subjective knowing in a feminist answer to Kantian denial of the female body.

A Tale of Love is centered around a complex and formal reworking of the scopic regime of film voyeurism. As Trinh T. Minh-ha argues:

Voyeurism runs through the history of love narrative, and voyeurism is here one of the threads that structure the "narrative" of the film. Is the film about love? Is it a love story? As the title suggests, it is above all a "tale"; a tale about the fiction of love in love stories and the process of consumption; a tale that marginalizes traditional narrative conventions such as action, plot, unity of time and realistic characters. Opening up a space where reality, memory and dream constantly pass into one another, A Tale of Love unfolds in linear and non-linear time. It offers both a sensual and an intellectual experience of film and can be viewed as a symphony of colors, sounds and reflections. As a character in the film says, "Narrative is a track of scents passed on from lovers to lovers."

Kieu acts as a foil to a multiplicity of desires embodied in the other characters. With Alikan, Minh, Java and Juliet, she experiences love through sight, sound, smell and touch. Similarly, the film offers the spectator more than one way into its own "love stories." Rather than being homogenized, the relationship between the visuals and the verses remains layered and elliptical. Light, setting, camera movement, sound and text all have a presence, a logic and a language of their own. Although they reflect upon one another, they are not intended to just illustrate the meanings of the narrative. The film also works with a subtly "denaturalized" space of acting. In the way the shots and the dialogues are carried out, both spectators and actors share the discomfort of voyeurism: the unnaturalness of those who "look without being looked at" (the makers, the spectators) versus the self-consciousness of those who "know they are being looked at while they are being watched." (Minh-ha 1995, press packet)

Kieu finds a form of subjectivity in that Imaginary realm described by Fredric Jameson where "a uniquely determinate configuration of space—one not yet organized around the individuation of [one's] own personal body" carries the spectator toward a "liquid perception," (355) or what Gilles Deleuze terms "the semi-subjective" (76). Kieu admits, for example, that she can no longer mention her namesake without feeling "somehow implied." Later she tells her friend Juliet that she feels as if she's living the tale of Kieu herself. At this point in the narrative, Kieu's perspective seems to melt between the void of the subjective and objective positionalities. The viewer is given few clues as to where Kieu's "reality" and "fantasy" sequences end or begin. We only view her writing and contemplating, as she is intercut with sequences in which she moves further and further toward self-knowledge and erotic mastery. In these sequences, as throughout the film, the musical accompaniment is composed of dissonant music and sounds, performed by the group the Construction of Ruins. This aural and visual dissonance is characteristic of postmodern feminist poetic transgressions. Rosi Braidotti characterizes such dissonance as one of the modes of expression of sexual difference; for Braidotti it implies a "nomadic quest for alternative representations of female feminist subjectivity" (135).

Kieu, who moves between the dissonant voice-overs of "The Tale of Kieu," her own narratives, her various levels of fantasy and her rerendering of "Kieu" acts as a subjectivity that reminds one of Deleuze and Guattari's *"devenir-femme"* (272). Kieu, as a "becoming woman" motions toward a multiplicity of subject positions. In rendering Kieu as the *devenir-femme*, Minh-ha uses many of the characteristic flourishes of her earlier films: her signature jump-cuts, disjunctive editing, extradiegetic voice-overs, repetitive bursts of music and voice, and post-structural disintegration of narrative time. Kieu's own voice-off is particularly dissonant, breaking the rules of off-screen knowledge in traditional film technique. If, as Pascal Bonitzer writes, "the voice-off is presumed to know" (324), Minh-ha renders Kieu's voice-off as that which instead *seeks to know, seeks to become*, and in a way supports Minh-ha's notion that the "filmic image becomes a *thinking* image" (1992, 263).

As Kieu hears snippets of "The Tale of Kieu," she conjures up fantasies of increasing self-inscription. She sees herself looking at a book of erotic photographs and she takes control of the photo-shoots with Alikan. In a signifying gesture of self-erotic becoming, she places the veils on herself and looks directly at the viewer and at the photographer. Next, she ridicules and interrogates Alikan: "A *headless* body. Women are not supposed to have a head, are they? . . . She is all flesh and body—*He* is the head, the mind, the thinking eye. That's nothing new, is it? Just look at the Egyptian Isis right up to Adam and Eve. *Women have always been made to lose their heads.*"

In a later sequence, Kieu fantasizes that the photographer himself is blind. This scene is perhaps an allusion to Brontë's *Wuthering Heights*, another love story in which the male protagonist figure is blinded by the woman author. Alikan is blinded by the masterly position of Kieu's becoming-subjectivity process. His blindness is as blind as psychoanalytic renderings of the feminine as lack. As Shoshana Felman writes, "To occupy a blind spot is not only to be blind, but in particular, to be blind to one's own blindness; it is to be unaware of the fact that one occupies a spot *within* the very blindness one seeks to demystify; that one is *in* madness, that one is always, necessarily, *in* literature" (199).

Kieu is now the *one-who-gazes*, and Alikan is grounded in a positionality of *to-be-looked-at-ness*. He finds the position painful, and he tells her to stop looking at him, because she's "hurting the story," perhaps by dislocating the center of the traditional romantic narrative. Kieu and Minh-ha do indeed "hurt the story," in the sense that they disallow its continued presence as a unified, monolithic, tragic, and binaristic love-tale, "interchangeable with any love tale." Minh-ha seeks to render this "love tale" as a fluid, multiplicitous, never-ending, and ever-varying series of tales. As Kieu tells her friend Juliet, near the end of the tale: "I haven't got just *one* story. I have several; all unfolding without a proper climax or an ending." Kieu thus orchestrates the manner in which the viewer views her tale, denying simplistic narrative construction. Her gaze returns the camera's gaze. She looks directly at the viewer at several key moments in her fantasy sequences, directly confronting voyeuristic pornographic representation. These gazes culminate in a fourth look, one that is described here by Paul Willemen:

What is at stake here is the "fourth look," as I have called it elsewhere. That is to say, any articulation of images and looks which brings into play the position and activity of the viewer as a distinctly separate factor also destabilizes that position and puts it at risk. All drives have active and passive facets and the scopic drive is no exception. When the scopic drive is brought into focus, then the viewer also runs the risk of *becoming the object of the look, of being overlooked in the act of looking.* (56)

As the object of the look, the viewer is inextricably bound to Alikan as viewer/viewed and to Kieu as tale-teller. The scopic lifting of the veil of narrative and spectatorship invokes an interactive specular regime that captures the viewer in the pleasures of the tales of Kieu. The viewer is implicated in the many narratives of Kieu, Kieu's fantasy sequences, and her mythmaking. An important facet in Kieu's reintegration of scopic selves is a fantasy of her meeting with her childlike self within several flashbacks and flashforwards in the film. The first few times Kieu imagines herself as a child—alone, naked. Later, she reimagines the fantasy with the child holding the hand of Kieu (as an adult). This is a fascinating reworking of what Teresa de Lauretis terms "the maternal imaginary of feminism" (1994, 165). Minh-ha's rendering of the maternal metaphor suggests a restaging of Kieu as a subject who undergoes loss and recovery of her own body that has been fragmented (decapitated by the voyeurism of Alikan). Here Kieu remaps and transcribes strategies of fetishism to acknowledge the libidinal loss of the integrated female body and to restage a primal scene of feminist psychoanalysis. Kieu's view of herself as self-gazing and self-knowing is a distinctively creative act, one that conjures the myth of psyche, where a woman's sexual and creative awakening are conjured through an imagination that combines both the rational and emotive sides of play and creativity. *The Tale of Kieu* emphasizes the importance of female fantasy, and, in turn, the importance of female interpreters. Kieu's remarks, fantasies and gazes confront us with the fact that she is a Vietnamese-American woman rereading a Vietnamese tale, or, as Tania Modleski reminds us "to read as a woman in patriarchal culture necessitates that the *hypothesis* of a woman reader be advanced by an *actual* woman reader: the female feminist critic" (133–34). The restaging of "The Tale of Kieu" in a twentieth-century feminist context is a brilliant location of a woman reader's recontextualization of the female text and the female body in culture.

MIRA NAIR

"To be mixed is the new world order"

BORN IN BHUBANESWAR, India, in 1957, and educated at Harvard University, Mira Nair is a cineaste of uncompromising feminist postcolonial subjectivity in-the-making. Nair's work explores the nomadic space of postmodern feminism, displacing the essentialism of the idea of "First" and "Third" Worlds. Recognizing that, as an Asian woman, she has been subject to the essentializing norms of colonialized subjectivity, Nair seeks to challenge and rupture the borders of identities based on class, race, gender, and location. Nair's nomadic identity, as an Indian filmmaker who lives in Africa, has had a liberating and formative impact on her choices as a filmmaker. In an interview with Janis Cole and Holly Dale, Nair speaks about her feelings toward the issues of home, displacement, and nomadism. As "a brown person, between black and white, I could move between these worlds very comfortably because I was neither" (149).

Nair's goal as an artist is distinctly political, yet she is completely at home when disrupting others' notions of political boundaries of politeness. She has taken criticism, for example, for her bleak portrayals of the lost and disenfranchised subalterns of her India. In *Jama Masjid Street Journal* (1979), a short diary/documentary (shot in black and white), Nair recorded Muslim men's reactions to her presence as a filmmaker in Delhi. This constituted a reversal of the traditional objectification of woman in film and photography as veiled object of gaze, thus claiming a site of an active and subjective female subaltern gaze.

So Far From India (1983) follows the grim journey of Ashok, an Indian immigrant, to New York who leaves his homeland to make better money to support his pregnant wife whom he has left in India. Nair records the grim deculturation of Ashok. In America, the film tells us, "You forget everything, who's your brother, who's your wife." Amit Shah applauded the cinéma vérité qualities in *So Far From India*, adding that the film records "the duality of the immigrant reality, the slow disintegration of rootedness, the new avenues and roadblocks of assimilation and belonging" (22).

Nair captures the multifacetedness of nomadic subjectivity, both the joy and pains, and everydayness of exile, here and later in *Mississippi Masala* (1991) and *The Perez Family* (1995). "My job is to provoke" (Cole and Dale 151), states Nair, and provoke she does with both *Salaam Bombay!* (1988) and *India Cabaret* (1986), masterpieces of documentary/narrative noir. *Salaam Bombay!* is a grim narrativist documentary, shot in cinéma vérité style, about the forgotten and destitute children, prostitutes, and drug addicts of Bombay. *India Cabaret*, a sobering ethnographical film on the lives of exotic dancers in India, was attacked by some Indian feminists on the basis that the film presented the women from the point of view of a "male gaze." As screenwriter Sooni Taraporevala observed:

> The main objections expressed were that the film presented a "male gaze," that it didn't bring out the exploitation and oppression of these women, that marriage was shown as the answer to a woman's condition, that the end was too optimistic, that the dancing in the film was too explicit and showed women as sex objects. (qtd. in Nair 66)

Mira Nair observes that these reactions represent a bias formed by Western feminist theoretical opinion. She comments that *India Cabaret* does not portray women as "essentially passive" (66). Nair points out the class-based and Western feminist based comment locates "a myopic view because it refuses to confront the dancers and the dance. . . . Not looking at the situation as it is will not make it disappear" (67). Perhaps what viewers find the most unsettling, Nair contends, is that "the women in it don't ask for our help, refuse to be viewed as victims, and do not need our pity" (67). The women in *India Cabaret* represent an example of the speaking subaltern who disrupts the assumption of Third World women as those who "rise above the debilitating generality of their 'object' status," the nonmonolithic subject recognized by Chandra Talpade Mohanty (71).

Perhaps unsurprisingly many Indian men were outspoken in their criticism of *India Cabaret*. At a screening in Hyderabad, at the International Film Festival in 1986, some men in the audience voiced their outrage at the film, because, as Nair concedes, "there were many men in the audience who would rather not hear, rather not recognize themselves as participants in the game of superiority over women. . . . They couldn't hide behind the refuge that fictional Indian cinema offers" (68).

One of the most astounding revelations of the film comes in Nair's handling of the men who patronize the clubs. The camera records their lengthy gazes at the women and their conversations about women as either whores or wives. *India Cabaret* unveils the commodification of women by recording the mundane transactions between the club owner, Suresh, and the dancers. In one disturbing moment, when one of the strippers manages to marry and thus get out of "the life," he repeatedly tries to get her to give her forwarding address. She refuses.

South Asians living in New York City prompted a ban by WNET (New York PBS) from showing *India Cabaret*. One letter, quoted by Nair, presented the view that only the "good" facets of India should be shown in the United States. The viewer felt that the station ought not present "a show about pornography from the viewpoint of the pornographer" (70). This attitude upholds "imperialism's image as the establisher of the good society marked by the espousal of the woman as *object* of protection from her own kind" as recognized by Gayatri Spivak (1988, 299).

Nair found this attitude even in her father, who also voiced his outrage that she make a film about women dancers, saying, "Scum—you are going to live with scum? . . . I know everything about these cabaret girls. They do anything for a quick buck" (Nair 62). Nair pushed him further. How did he know about such "scum?" Nair then discovered that one of her father's friends had "offered" a cabaret girl to him. Recognizing the obvious double standard at work in this situation, Nair asked her father "How do you regard your friend?" (Nair 62), to which he had no reply. The words of Vasanti, one of the dancers in *India Cabaret*, also disrupt such a double standard, "If the viewer does not feel shame, why should I feel shame?" she says, directly to the audience.

Nair brings forth the active subjectivities of women as speaking subalterns in *India Cabaret* by foregrounding identity in first-person-address, in the "naming" of her subjects (and underscoring names with intertitles—Lovina, Rekha, Rosi, Vassanti) and in the manner in which she avoids the disembodied knowledge of the standard documentary voice-over. In *India Cabaret*, the dancers speak directly to the audience; telling their own stories, witnessing failures and joys and their very corporeality. In one of the opening shots, Lovina flirts with the gaze of the camera as she applies her makeup. Rekha tells us of her dancing ability in a distinctively bragging tone, then explains the double standard toward strippers, "Everybody goes to cabarets but won't admit it."

Rekha's feminist revision of a well-known fable is well worth repeating because of its deft creation of feminist mythmaking, even and especially in the face of economic and cultural attempts at her own erasure as "scum":

Then Yamaraj, you know, The Lord of Death, he took 3 women up at the same time. He asked them, "What sins have you committed on earth?" The first woman said, "Sir, I did not sin. I loved one man, I left him and married another man. After marriage, I did not even look at any other man."

"Give her the silver gates!" The Lord said.

So she went to heaven through silver gates. Then the second woman came. "What did you do down there?" The Lord asked.

"Sir, I loved only one man and married the same man. After marriage, I did not look at any other man in the eye.' "

"Give her the golden gates!" The Lord commanded.

Last came a cabaret dancer. "What were your sins?" asked the Lord of Death.

"Sir, down there I made no man unhappy. I gave pleasure to every man, to every man I brought ecstasy. To all the men in the world I brought happiness."

"Give her the keys to my room!" The Lord said. "Down there you made so many men happy, now up here you can make me happy too."

What did the virtuous virgins get? One got a lousy silver door. The other got a lousy golden door. Only Rekha got the keys to the Lord himself! (Nair 58)

Rekha's remaking of herself as a mythic Goddess of "privilege" though phallogocentrically defined is undeniably self-affirming.

Rekha is aware of her commodification, in a system that sees her as a "polluted" *raat ki raanis* by night, and a mother, sister, *ayah*, an ordinary woman by day. Yet Rekha refuses to be invisible, refuses to be objectified by an ethnographic gaze. Her knowledge is distinctively bodied and underscored by the presence of her body language. She tells us the fable as she glares at us, smoking, laughing, gesturing, refusing the mantle of the polluted subaltern. Hers is a "body-in-action" (11), as described by Bill Nichols, who contends that the ethnographer subjectifies herself with such action: "To act is to affirm or construct an identity, and to identify with such a process is to forge an identity bound up with this very act, a sense of self as being-in-action" (12).

The embodied knowledge of Rekha thus maps uncharted space for diasporic self-knowledge. Mira Nair's presentation of such knowledge moves beyond traditional ethnographic practice, avoiding political dogmatism in favor of a fantasy of self-inscription. Nair achieves an act of genuine performative feminism in this film, and she does so from a space of self-knowledge and class-perspective. Operating from an educated, more "safe" middle-class position, she never patronizes her subjects and manages "not to present them either as passively oppressed or full of hidden virtues," as noted by Amit Shah (24).

In a letter discussing *India Cabaret* quoted by Nair, one viewer praised the film, finding it "never polemic," adding "nor is it voyeuristic." This viewer found *India Cabaret* to be a postcolonialist answer to the images of India as "romanticized empire" seen in "oft-repeated travelogues and quaint memoirs" (Nair 70). *India Cabaret* won the award for Best Documentary at the Global Village Film Festival in New York, the Golden Athena at the Athens International Film Festival, and the Blue Ribbon at the American Film Festival in 1986. It is regularly screened at many international film venues, particularly women's film festivals.

Nair's penchant for championing the underprivileged classes and, in particular, economically deprivileged women, is consistently a center of her film projects. Her 1985 documentary, *Children of Desired Sex* looks at the misuse of sex-determination tests that quite often lead to female foeticide in India. *Children of a Desired Sex* is another example of Nair's ability to bring controversial subject matter to the public eye. She consistently maps spaces for those who are culturally invisible.

Nair operates from a postcolonial feminist rhetorical space, one that speaks for the dislocated exiles of inequality toward class, gender, race, ability, nationality, age, and sexual orientation. Her feminist rhetoric is not limited to addressing women's circumstances alone, and her ethos is one of "empathetic knowing," as described by the feminist philosopher Lorraine Code: "Responsible, empathetic knowing will start from a recognition that mutuality can never be assumed, but it can sometimes be realized, not just between two people, but by extending a second-person mode into even wider contexts" (142).

Empathetic knowing is an important concept to talk about within the context of current debates about who can speak for whom. Empathetic knowledge fosters border crossings and "resists closure, invites conversation, and fosters and requires second- person relations" (Code 126). Above all, empathetic knowledge can be a tool for rupturing hegemonically perceived power/knowledge relationships, especially those defined by outmoded terms such as "Third World" and "First World," for example.

Certainly cultural and historical determiners must be kept in mind when making or talking about films on the "culturally invisible," the culturally silenced and politically oppressed subalterns of the world; but cultural/historical knowledge must not be repositioned as a new frontier/border or silencing mechanism itself. My comments here are in reaction to the current climate in academic circles that moves toward silencing discussion around postcolonial feminist issues and projects. In particular, I am positioning myself against a political position that seeks to perpetuate the binarisms between "First" and

"Third" Worlds of filmmaking practice. My remarks are intended to foster a discourse that disrupts these categories and many of the received notions on their usefulness. I argue here that Mira Nair's films, in particular *Salaam Bombay!*, should be considered as a rupturing signifier to the categories of First and Third World filmmaking.

Salaam Bombay! is a narrative fiction film that uses specific tropes of the narrative feature film to voice the marginalized figures who are so often rendered voiceless in colonialist ethnographies. In addition, Nair uses elements of cinéma vérité to imbue the film with a metanarrative of the real. She shoots in actual locations on Bombay streets, she uses non-actors, her lighting and mise-en-scène are naturalistic and stylistically underscored by her documentary background. It is important to remember, however, that the film is a fictional narrative designed to provoke empathy among viewers toward homeless children, prostitutes, drug addicts, and young women from Nepal who are forced into prostitution and commodification through the flesh trade of Bombay.

The narrative of *Salaam Bombay!* is seen through the child's gaze in the form of the character Chaipau, a young boy who leaves home and goes to the city (Bombay) to make enough money to extricate himself from the trouble he caused by taking his brother's bicycle. The tragedy of Chaipau is that, as the viewer suspects, he will never be able to return home because he is inexorably drawn into a colonial urban nightmare of economic exploitation. The viewer identifies with Chaipau's struggles. More importantly, perhaps, is the fact that Chaipau empathizes with those around him whom he views being pressed into prostitution, drugs, and a complex system of capitalist exploitation.

Chaipau's gaze functions as a signifier of those who would ignore or misperceive the suffering and oppression of the homeless, the lost drug-dependent dealers, the women forced into prostitution and bondage. Chaipau's gaze supersedes any question of "First" vs. Third World. He is not only interchangeable with "any oppressed Third World subject" (295), as Arora concedes, but he is interchangeable with any modern homeless urban figure. His story takes place in a "Third" World city, however, he is a fictional construct who can essentially be seen as a stand-in for the homeless person in any modern city. His gaze demands a multiplicity of viewing positions, and Nair repeatedly cross-identifies him with oppressed women (prostitutes and children) through eye-matches and gazes that lead the viewer (whether from New York City, Bombay, or London) to involve themselves in the embodied subjectivities of the fictional constructs.

Chaipau involves the viewer in the lives of Chillum, the lost drug-addicted pusher and Sweet Sixteen, a Nepalese teen-age girl who is sold into slavery/"marriage." The film also encourages cross-identification with a very young girl and her mother, a prostitute. Chaipau's recognition of the commodification of women transcends cultural borders and questions around the definition of "First/Third" World. Certainly the socioeconomic conditions of the commodification of women and the commodification of individuals involved in the drug trade has important specificity with regard to the city of Bombay, however, Nair makes the viewer aware of at least some of these particulars. In one sequence Chillum sells drugs to a white (American) tourist and the "First" World figure is ridiculed as an object. Here Nair is turning the gaze of the supposed "First" World back upon itself. The Indian man has contempt for the tourist, and by extension, contempt for the corrupt capitalist system of the drug trade.

But it is the passages of the film that present the prostitute and her daughter which, at least for this viewer, have the greatest resonance. Their scenes are compelling because they spend time together singing and sleeping side-by-side. The young girl's acceptance and understanding of her mother's position is hampered by her youth. She continually interrupts her mother during paid sex by clawing at the window outside her cramped room. Though marginalized, these two figures have hope because they share a community and they find joy in one another's company despite the brutal realities around them. Nair demonstrates their capacity for survival to bring forth their subjectivities. They are multifaceted individuals, despite their label as the "scum" or the "polluted" underbelly of Bombay society. Later, when the bureaucratic officials take away the child from her mother, stating that she is unfit, the viewer, any viewer, must see this as an act against women, a further erasure of the underclass, which ultimately leads to genocide. Any system that seeks to destroy an already deprivileged family is a system that perpetuates the murder of children. The child, we know, will end up on the street, or worse, sold into marriage. The mother no longer has a will to live, therefore this is a system of sanctioned murder whereby women are doubly persecuted both by virtue of gender and economic oppression.

Even if *Salaam Bombay!* were "constructed for, and subject to, the gaze of the First World" as Arora claims (296), any feminist would agree that this film is calling for an end to the international systematic oppression of women, particularly the regulated persecution of prostitutes. As in *India Cabaret*, Nair is unafraid to speak for the women who work in the flesh business. The commodification of women is underscored in *Salaam Bombay!* by the always-watching gaze of the young Chaipau, who records what happens to the women around him. Even though the main narrative of the film would seem to be Chaipau's fall and degradation as a tea-boy, I'd suggest that the film's metanarrative is the struggle of women, from girlhood to enslavement. The evidence that I bring to such a statement is that Nair and the screenwriter, Sooni Taraporevala, weave together Chaipau's story with the narrative of the young Nepalese girl, who is kidnapped, kept as a virgin, and sold with the story of the older prostitute. Both are made false promises by Baba, the drug-runner and pimp who routinely abuses men and women alike. Baba, we learn, promised the prostitute that he would marry her if she had his child. Instead, he has kept her in servitude.

As a parallel narrative, Baba is introduced to the young virgin "Sweet Sixteen," a recently kidnapped Nepalese girl. He also promises to take her away from this life. Instead, she is sold to an old man by a vicious woman slave trader. Chaipau sees all this, and he tries to help Sweet Sixteen to no avail. Baba's misogyny is further underscored by an incident in which he whips Chillum brutally to frighten a white British journalist who has come to speak with him (for reasons unknown to the viewer). Why does Nair include this scene? Is it to level criticism at the white privileged colonialist interloper? Is it to invite cross-cultural anger at brutality toward women? Perhaps it can be read as another indictment of the white woman's colonial gaze?

This eruption of cruel cinema conjures images from ethnographic practice, such as that of Jean Rouch or Luis Buñuel. However, Nair's cruel cinema is rendered through a postcolonial feminist gaze and is therefore a critique of the gaze of the "First" world, as I'd define it, the gaze of privilege. *Salaam Bombay!* attacks "white privilege and its looking relations," as described by Jane Gaines. Nair's film moves Gaines' theory into practice by criticizing, even disallowing, the cultural denial of the black female body in terms of dominant white feminism, which, according to Gaines theorizes "the female image in terms of objectification, fetishization, and symbolic absence [while] their Black counterparts describe the body as a site of symbolic resistance and the 'paradox of nonbeing' " (209).

Far from universalizing women's experiences, *Salaam Bombay!* particularizes the unique cultural experiences of (fictional) women of Bombay in an effort both to engage in meaningful rendition of subjectivity and form alliances among women of similar, but not essentialized, positions across small borders (Hindu culture/Nepalese culture) and larger borders (prostitutes and women commodified in cities as disparate as Bombay and London).

Cinema practice, especially in fiction, works toward universalizing the fictional constructs of those who dwell on the fringes of society. It is precisely for this reason that Nair chose to move into fiction filmmaking. Like Trinh T. Minh-ha, Nair moved from documentary to fiction because, she says, "I felt that a fiction camera could get into these otherwise out of bounds spaces, much, much better than a hidden camera would" (Cole and Dale 147).

Salaam Bombay! was made despite almost unprecedented adversity, especially funding problems. Nair fought for funding and initially found support from Britain's Channel 4. She later secured funds from the National Film Development Corporation of India, and, despite the reluctance to support a feature film by an Indian woman director, she made the film for about four hundred and fifty thousand dollars, a minuscule budget for such a massive undertaking, with its many set-ups and extensive location shooting. Nair's ability to film *Salaam Bombay!* on such a limited budget in a limited period of time is truly impressive. Her extensive experience in documentary most certainly prepared her, to some extent, for the job.

Salaam Bombay! was received with tremendous international acclaim at the Directors' Fortnight at the Cannes Film Festival. Nair won the Camera D'Or for best first feature, the Prix du Publique for most popular film at Cannes, and *Salaam Bombay!* went on to receive an Academy Award nomination for Best Foreign Language Film. Mira Nair was courted by Hollywood executives after the success of *Salaam Bombay!*, however, as Nair says, she was not happy with the manner in which Hollywood wished to "whiten" her projects. "At first everybody wanted me to do white things, and white issues" Nair told Cole and Dale (149). Nevertheless, Nair began pre-production for *Mississippi Masala*, a film about people of color, particularly exile cultures, and the issues of home, cultural displacement, and intercultural romance. Nair felt inspired by her own experience as a student at Harvard as a "brown person in between black and white" (Cole and Dale 149).

Nair became interested particularly in the Asian expulsion from Uganda and in the Indian immigrant population in the South of the United States. She began to rethink the notion of exile, and began to conceive of a story that interwove the experiences of Indians who were thrown out of Africa because they were not black, and African-Americans, who were born in America, yet had never been to Africa. Nair and screenwriter Sooni Taraporevala began to develop a screenplay that traces the story of the Loha family who are forced out of Uganda in the 1970s. They resettle in Greenwood, Mississippi, but lose their class status in the United States, where they are pushed into the lower rung of the immigrant population, and work for a more affluent Indian family who run a chain of motels.

Nair told Andrea Stuart that *Mississippi Masala* offered her an opportunity to explore the relationship between Asian and African-American people: "I wanted to explore what would happen if a member of one community crossed the border of colour into another . . . to explore exile, memory, nostalgia, dislocation: This thing we call home" (212). Made for about six million dollars, *Mississippi Masala* stars Sarita Choudhury and Denzel Washington as the young lovers who cross borders of black and brown communities in a star-crossed love affair that brings a colonial narrative to postcolonial issues. While the dominant narrative of *Mississippi Masala* is centered around Mina and De-metrius, it could be argued that *Mississippi Masala* employs a superficially constructed Hollywood love story actually to voice a political narrative of exiled Indian people who were forced out of Uganda under the regime of Idi Amin. This counternarrative strategy, in turn, resituates the film as a contemplation of issues found in Nair's earlier documentary films: exile, difference, and the border crossings of African and Asian diasporic communities.

The counternarratives of *Mississippi Masala* can be located in the gaze of Mina, in a manner not unlike that of the gaze of young Chaipau in *Salaam Bombay!* and Rekha in *India Cabaret*. It is through Mina's eyes that we experience the embodied knowledge of difference, exile, and diasporic culture. *Mississippi Masala* brings a documentarist's notion of truth-claims to a stylized narrative that is palatable to audiences seeking Hollywood-style narrative pleasure. While marketable as an interracial love story, one that celebrates the exotic Other (the spicy Masala), the film actually problematizes black/brown issues and is critical of a simplistic celebration of Otherness. By grounding *Mississippi Masala* at the borders of documentary and fiction, Nair subverts colonial film practice and undermines the Hollywood romance.

By shooting on location in Uganda, and by telling the story of Indians forced out of Africa, Nair maps colonial history through a manner described by Aparna Dharwadker: " . . . fictions can work precisely to neutralize or repudiate the figurations of institutional history and can serve as alternative sources of historical knowledge . . . " (44). *Mississippi Masala* moves at the borders of truth-claim between fiction and documentary, in order to speak to ideologically resistant audiences as well as to postcolonial-minded viewers. At the center of the narrative, the viewer is faced with the economic and political conditions of exile and moved away from superficial treatments of migrant populations from Africa and India.

The film caters to an audience eager to celebrate exotic Otherness in the form of sexuality between brown bodies. It is marketed as a celebration of diversity, yet it delivers a political examination of race and colonialism as they have been positioned in Western filmic practice. This is an instance of resistance to colonialism, which, according to Thomas Foster, engages in "developing political possibilities that cannot be conceived within the bounds of a colonialist system" (67).

Mississippi Masala conceives a utopic space where black/brown alliances overcome cultural difference and colonialist economic conditions, a space where exile is not necessarily tragic, where race and class does not always dictate economic agency. At the same time, there is a dialogic voice in the film that criticizes disunity between people of color, the Dystopic realities of white oppression, and the perpetuation of economic exploitation of people of color. The first hint that *Mississippi Masala* isn't a mere love story is that it opens with a flashback to war-torn Uganda in 1972. Here Jay, an Indian lawyer (played by Roshan Seth) and his African friend Okelo (played by Konga Mbandu) are harassed by military police. Their friendship is displaced by Idi Amin's order that all Asians must leave the country. Okelo reiterates the philosophy behind Amin's orders, "Africa is for Africans: Black Africans."

The viewer sees this through young Mina's point-of-view. Mina observes a tragedy of forced exile and the mechanics of militarist regimes that rips apart Asian/African relationships and cause so much pain to her family. As Mina watches, her family is forced onto a bus, and her mother is taken off the bus at gunpoint by a military police officer. After humiliating her and threatening her life, he returns her to the bus. At this point in the film, we see the tragedy of exile through Mina's eyes, but the film rapidly moves us to Greenwood, Mississippi, 1990, where Mina's mother owns a liquor shop in a predominantly Black neighborhood.

Mina's mother seems to have largely recovered from the hardships of forced immigration; however, Mina's father is obsessed with the past. He continues to seek the return of his land by suing the Ugandan government. His family exists at the threshold between cultures, the "liminal state." As described by Hamid Naficy, the "liminal state" of exile is both positive and negative. Produced when exiled people are denied a sense of home and identity through a disruption of status, rank, and property, the liminality of exilehood "not only causes paralysis and deterioration, but also it positions the exiles to play and to reterritorialize themselves, i.e., build themselves anew" (Naficy 85–86). The narrative of *Mississippi Masala* allows Jay to rebuild his life after a long period of paralysis. He is pushed to the brink of change by Mina's interracial affair with Demetrius. Similarly, Demetrius is able to extrapolate himself from economic reliance on white bankers when he loses his livelihood when the bankers rescind the loan that supports his rug-cleaning business because of his relationship with Mina.

It is Mina herself who explores the liminality of exile both by her actions and words. Mina's liminality allows her the gaze of one who is able to "question the 'common sense' of both home and host cultures and to reconfigure them in ways that potentially either threaten or enrich both" (Naficy 87). Mina's movements across cultural lines give her a heightened awareness of race/gender/class issues from a postcolonial perspective. By embracing her liminal subject positionality, Mina uses it to foster her self-inscription as a sexually independent outlaw figure. Along the way, she observes the critical distance common to liminality and is unafraid of making the people around her aware of her powerful and subversive presence.

Mina's enunciative and performative acts disrupt the trajectory of the arranged marriage that has been planned by her parents. Her father and mother are anxious for her to marry a wealthy light-skinned Asian, Harry, but Mina falls for an African-American man (Demetrius) and refuses to abide by her parents' wishes. Mina sees some of her parents' values as old-fashioned, class, race, and gender-determined. "Face it ma—you gotta darkie daughter," she says to her mother. Mina pursues her love-object, Demetrius, despite her family's wishes that she marry Harry and stay "with her own kind." Through Mina's perspective, Nair observes racism, sexism, and classism in the Asian, African-American, and Southern white communities. An Indian gossip, played by Nair herself, observes the political complexities of skin color within the Asian community: "You can be dark and have money. You can be fair and have no money, but you can't be dark and have no money and expect to get Harry!" The complexity of racism pervades all three communities in *Mississippi Masala*. Though an Asian hotel owner proclaims "all of us people of color should stick together," he is merely mouthing the saying. In actuality, he holds bigoted views about African-Americans.

The disharmony between black and brown communities bubbles under the surface until the relationship between Demetrius and Mina is discovered. The Asian and African-American communities know little about one another. For example, Demetrius' partner, Tyrone, insists on referring to Mina as Mexican. Mina's exile status is the object of much questioning at the dinner table when Demetrius brings her home to meet his family. Is she Native American Indian?

they wonder. Is she African? Her identity under scrutiny, Mina explains that her family migrated from Africa, but they are Asian. Demetrius' family asks her why there are Indians in Africa, and Mina explains how the British colonists used Asians to build the railways in Africa. "Kinda like slaves?" Demetrius' brother asks. A member of the family then pursues this link with the African-American disaporic community, observing that "We are from Africa, but we have never been there."

Mina's family reacts with horror when they learn about her relationship with an African-American. Her parents accuse her of bringing shame upon the family. They cannot conceive of integrating Demetrius into the family and the Asian community. Indeed, the Asian and African communities, though they share many common values, are culturally exiled from one another. They are isolated by cultural practice and by an economic system that deprivileges them and discourages them from creating bonds across the Asian/African-American diasporas. The white bankers leap at any opportunity to disenfranchise people of color; they immediately cut off Demetrius' bank loan at the slightest hint of impropriety. Mina's mother fears that she will lose business at her liquor store, and Mina's father almost loses his job at the motel. Nair demonstrates exactly how people of color are objects of routine discrimination and how the Southern white hegemony holds the keys to economic power and free enterprise. Mina and Demetrius flee the South leaving their families in order to be together, thus demonstrating the manner in which diasporic cultures are torn apart by the politics of racism.

It's interesting to note how Nair and Taraporevala imbue *Mississippi Masala* with elements borrowed directly from experience. Nair left India when she was only nineteen. As an exile, she began to understand the economics of British colonization. Nair observed firsthand the experience of the colonization process whereby Asians are colonized and forced into poverty and exile. As they move to other countries, Asians and Eurasians tend to do well as merchants, but they serve to uphold the privileged few and are often resented by the older working class communities. In the American South, Asians bought many of the hotels, sometimes angering the African-Americans who had lived there for several generations. Nair told Samuel Freedman, in an interview in the *New York Times*, that she saw blatant racism when she went to South Carolina to research the phenomena of Indian motel chains. Nair described the situation: "There's a tension around the issue of alliances. The black folks think, 'All of us people of color must stick together.' And the Indians cash in on that when it suits them. But the white people are glad the middle class isn't black" (14).

In the film, Demetrius voices this nascent tension and anger between African-American and Indian communities: "I know that folks can come to this country and be as black as the ace of spades, but soon as they come here they start to act white—and treat us like their doormats." Demetrius' outburst is indicative of the conflict between black and brown cultures in the United States. Nair draws a parallel between this particular conflict and that of Asians and Africans in Africa in the 1970s. Though the film celebrates melange cultures, hybrid cultures, and mixedness, Nair avoids falsely determined utopic visions of interracial harmony. Instead, she explores the boundaries of exile cultures that are both difficult and at times harmonious. Andrea Stuart comments that "*Mississippi Masala* is no rainbow coalition tract" (214). Ultimately Demetrius and Mina are forced into self-exile and become migrants because of their relationship, and similarly Asian/African friendships in Uganda are thrown into exile and hardship. Perhaps even more provocative, however, is Nair's treatment of whites as absent peripheral characters. "I wanted the white characters to be absent" (Stuart 214), Nair explains. The characterization of white as absence has the effect of bringing the African-American and Asian communities into the foreground. It also reverses Hollywood filmic representation of people of color as absence, lack, or peripheral stereotypes.

The few incidences in *Mississippi Masala* that include white presence depict white Southern folks as mean-spirited, stingy, racist, or stupid in a manner that is designed as a visual shorthand of whiteness that is constructed for the pleasure of Black and Brown spectatorship. It is worth examining these brief glimpses of these stereotypes of dominant white culture because they display truths usually reserved for documentary films rather than romantic narratives.

The few times that Nair shows us a glimpse of white presence, she usually cuts to an insert in which white people are harshly criticizing African-Americans or Asians. For example, one insert shows two white shop clerks complaining about the noise of a nearby Asian wedding. Their accents and expressions mark them as ignorant and racist. "I wish they'd go back to the reservation," says the older man. In another shot, two white women who were apparently supportive toward Demetrius when he needed a bank loan observe Demetrius and his brother. "He's the *good* one," one of the women says—demonstrating the white American practice of separating African-Americans into Good/Bad binarisms based on little more than prejudice and privilege. Later on, when Demetrius is discovered having an interracial love affair with Mina, these same white women are the first to phone the bank to withdraw their support from Demetrius—Demetrius is no longer viewed as the "good Black."

Demetrius and his business partner, Tyrone, are called into the bank to hear that they will be losing their bank loan. In this scene, Nair presents us with a smarmy white loan officer who drones on about how he worked hard for his stature and expects them (African-Americans) to work as hard. As he speaks, he is constructed as a boastful, vicious, and privileged caricature of the Southern old (white) boy network. An ostentatious electronic photocube sits at his desk, revolving to exhibit his family photographs. From Demetrius's subjective point of view, we hear him droning on about what one needs to secure a business loan: "character, credit, collateral, capital . . . " As Demetrius and Tyrone leave the man's office, Demetrius finishes the sentence sarcastically: "Yeah—character, credit, collateral and *color.*" Nair uses white presence to articulate African-American and Asian routine economic and social hardship at the hands of white privilege, and also to demonstrate the manner in which white Americans support a system that serves to manipulate, dominate, and separate people of color. For example, when the news of Mina and Demetrius hits the hotel gossip circuit, we catch a glimpse of an old white Southerner on the phone with one of Mina's family. "Are y'all havin' nigger troubles?" he says with a Southern drawl. The statement, designed to manipulate the Asian hotel clerk into a false position of privilege as an insider and as a white person comes from the same white man who, earlier in the film, called for Indians to "go back to the reservation." Thus Nair exposes the manipulation of exiled migrant people of color by exposing the machinations of white Southerners. These moments have the veracity of truth-claims usually found in more formal cinéma vérité, and they are also extended to brief insets of American television culture, which occasionally shows its white presence in *Mississippi Masala.* Nair demonstrates, for example, how one Asian hotel clerk falls prey to the get-rich-quick television personality "Dave Deldado." Wealth, pleasure, and insider status are indelibly tied to pursuit of money and whiteness in the television presence of Deldado. This is accomplished in the film in the briefest of asides, yet it underscores Nair's rhetoric of white presence through absence, her criticism of white privilege through brief glimpses of cinéma vérité drawn from the landscape of American television culture.

Though little has been written on Asian-American spectatorship, Jacqueline Bobo's work on black female spectatorship can certainly be useful in underscoring the importance of Black and Indian viewing positions of *Mississippi Masala.* Nair's critique of white supremacy is designed with a mixed audience in mind; it appeals to both Indian women and African-American women as a romance with strongly drawn political subtexts. It delivers a romance, but more than that, it unmasks the politics of white racist Southern society. Like those Black filmmakers identified by Jacqueline Bobo who "have taken on the task of creating images of themselves different from those continually reproduced in traditional works" (Bobo 45), Nair similarly creates fresh images of people of color and critical images of whiteness in *Mississippi Masala*.

Mississippi Masala appeals to Black spectators, both through its narrative pleasures and its visual effects and the use of music. Nair worked closely with her cinematographer, Ed Lachman, to find the most pleasing and effective lighting designs to portray black and brown flesh. Nair became interested in the lack of knowledge around filming black skin, stating, "No one seemed to question the fact that Hollywood cinematography is designed to flatter one particular group" (Stuart 215). Nair's attention to Blackness supports her position as a champion of black spectatorial pleasure. The soundtrack of *Mississippi Masala* is a pleasurable melange of African, Indian, African-American, and worldbeat music that provides bridges across Black and Brown cultures. The audience is treated to African chorals and instrumentals, African-American blues and rap music, Indian wedding songs and reggae music. Nair's choice of actors for the film is also in keeping with the needs and desires of Black spectatorial pleasure. Denzel Washington is not just any topnotch African-American actor, he is a veritable heartthrob in the African-American female community. Sharmila Tagore is well known to Asian women from working in Indian musicals. Roshan Seth, who has worked for the Royal Shakespeare Company, is a figure with whom both Asians and Blacks of the diaspora can identify. *Mississippi Masala* garnered a great deal of critical praise and a fairly wide release. Like films by other Black women filmmakers, *Mississippi Masala* is designed to meet the needs of Black spectatorship. Like *Daughters of the Dust*, it documents American social fabric in a way described here by Jacqueline Bobo:

> [These] works provide a coping mechanism, enabling Black women to recognize the array of forces controlling their lives. And their cultural texts, in conjunction with other factors, prompt Black women to act to change the negative conditions impeding their advancement. In a sort of symbiotic relationship, Black women's texts nourish and sustain their readers. (6)

For her next film, *The Perez Family*, Mira Nair moved on to study the lives of immigrant exiles from Cuba. *The Perez Family* is a love story that uncovers the lives of Cuban refugees who fled to Miami in 1980, and starred Angelica Houston and Alfred Malign. Like *Mississippi Masala*, *The Perez Family* uses the standard Hollywood romance formula as a tableau to stage political critique and to embody the visual pleasure of people of color, although it did not enjoy the resounding critical or commercial success of *Mississippi Masala.* Nair lives in Africa with her husband, Mahmood Kampala, and their son Zohran. She continues to work between Hollywood, Africa and India. As she told Janis Cole and Holly Dale, "I'm one of those hybrids that has a foot in both worlds" (153). As a documentarist, she has made some of her finest work. As a fiction film- maker, she is forging a new hybrid aesthetic. As a woman from India and Africa and the African and Asian diaspora, Nair speaks from a space of exile discourse that affords her a uniquely privileged space of identity. As Nair notes of her own work and identity, "I come from a place of personal filmmaking" (Cole and Dale 150).

❖ 8 ❖

OTHER VOICES

WOMEN FILMMAKERS OF the African and Asian diaspora seek spaces of agency and creative energy where "cultural agency opens up—and holds together—the performative and pedagogic" (Bhabha 1994, 155), thus "revealing and linking Black spaces that have been separated and suppressed by White times" (Diawara 1993, 13). The importance of subjectivity and the reclamation of space constitute one common determiner in films of the African and Asian diaspora. This chapter will celebrate the reclamation of space and female subjectivity in the films of many women film directors of the diaspora, however, the reader should keep in mind that this section is *absolutely not* meant to constitute a canonized, exclusionary, or even a comprehensive sisterhood. It is, instead, just a sampling of the many women directors of color who are directing films either independently or through the Hollywood system.

Michelle Parkerson

Black lesbian filmmaker Michelle Parkerson was born and raised in Washington, D.C. Her first film was *Sojourn*, which she made as a student at Temple University. Parkerson is best known for her documentaries on Black women artists: *But Then, She's Betty Carter, Sweet Honey in the Rock*, and *Stormé: The Lady of the Jewel Box*. Greg Tate summarized Parkerson's evolution as a film director:

> Parkerson's passion for film was inculcated by the first Black woman she ever loved—her mother. "My mother was the first person who turned me on to really scrutinizing film. She knew all the directors' names, knew the names and importance of the costume designers, actors, actresses. I learned a lot about the awesome power of film over the spectator from her and to associate names with what I was looking at in terms of craft. My mother made a big effort to point out Dorothy Dandridge to me. That made a big difference in my life, recognizing that this Black woman was doing something that hadn't been done, was a Black first. Watching the March on Washington and the killing of Lee Harvey Oswald over Cheerios one morning were two tele-events that left

a lasting impression. The way media embosses imagery, i.e., history on our minds, was stamped on me at those two points." . . . Parkerson credits the '60s news show *Black Journal* with instilling the belief that she could become a filmmaker, not least because of producer/director **Madeline Anderson** (according to Parkerson's research, the first Black woman to work behind the camera since '30s evangelist **Eloice Gist** and **Zora Neale Hurston**). She remembers being especially impressed with the work of **St. Claire Bourne**'s program on her father's church, the United Church of Christ, *Let the Church Say Amen.* Having spent umpteen years as a documentarian, Parkerson now finds herself compelled to deploy the powers of imagination present in her fiction and poetry. (1991, 77)

Parkerson's support of the black women's filmmaking community has been as much a part of her creative endeavors as her filmmaking. She's credited as an outspoken activist, teacher, and mentor to emerging women filmmakers of color. Michelle Parkerson has also been particularly active as a researcher in Black women's film culture. She has been instrumental in mining the film archives and early periodicals for evidence of African-American women's participation. Parkerson told David Nicholson in 1986:

We are unearthing a lot of history. Many of us are about the business of documenting black women's experience. . . . There has been a recognition, not large, and not in proportion to the talent of black women filmmakers—but I think there is beginning to be a recognition of our presences behind the camera. (1986a, 55)

Michelle Parkerson's documentaries embody black female subjectivity at its most basic. Here, black women speak for themselves. *Stormé*, for example, is a refreshing documentary on a crossdressing African-American woman who tells her own story as a member of the legendary Jewel Box Revue. Stormé's knowledge and subjectivity are distinctively embodied (rather than disembodied by a traditional voice-over) because she/he tells her/his own story.

Jackie Shearer

Jackie Shearer is another early documentarist of the African-American filmmaking diaspora. Shearer worked on *Eyes on the Prize* and later worked in documentary for PBS's *The American Experience*. Shearer's film work covers some of the same historical territory as the Hollywood feature film, *Glory*, which treated the experience of the 54th Regiment of Black soldiers. According to Greg Tate, "Shearer's segment reveals that the real men of the 54th were more educated and assured of their manhood than *Glory* portrayed them to be." As Shearer told Tate, she entered the film industry after a background in political activism: "I knew I didn't have the temperament for organizing, but I liked the idea of media as a political tool since it had been an effective tool for socialization against me. I wanted to master an enslaving technology for empowering uses" (1991, 77).

Shearer moved into narrative filmmaking with *Addie and the Pink Carnations*, a tale set in the 1930s that follows the story of a Black woman who moves north and faces racism in her travails. As Shearer explains, she wished to rectify historical omissions and misperceptions in the film; she wished to show that Black women were:

> autonomous, strong, kickass women who did not sacrifice their own mothering responsibilities to raise white women's children. . . . One of the things I'd like to do in *Addie* is break up the narrative with little documentary nuggets. It might be jarring to some people, but I like being jarred myself. I don't know whether to ascribe that to being Black and female and growing up in the projects. (Tate 1991, 77)

Kathleen Collins

African-American Kathleen Collins (full name Kathleen Conway Collins Prettyman) was born on March 18, 1942, and grew up in Jersey City, New Jersey. After graduating from Skidmore, she did graduate work in Paris. Collins was a writer of plays, screenplays, and fiction. From 1967 to 1974, she worked as a film editor for NET and Williams Greaves Productions. She was active as a filmmaker and she taught at City College of New York. In 1979 Collins completed production of *The Cruz Brothers* on a tiny budget of $5,000. *The Cruz Brothers* concerns three Puerto Rican brothers. Collins was discouraged when she was criticized for making a film about people from a different culture, but the film did well and Collins was able to secure funds for *Losing Ground* (1982), her next film project. During the filming of *Losing Ground*, Collins was diagnosed with cancer. She died of cancer just after the completion of *Gouldtown* (1988), a film about a long-established settlement of African-Americans.

Collins was outspoken on her feelings about the need for Black women to tell their stories on film as part of a "redemptive process" necessary to achieve change. She also felt that race comes before gender in political struggles, "to separate oneself from black men is to allow America the final triumph of division," she said in an interview with David Nicholson (1986b, 17). Collins leaves behind a legacy of great importance to African-American cinema. She is often, like Michele Parkerson, mentioned as an important mentor figure in many interviews with black women directors.

Ayoka Chenzira

Ayoka Chenzira comes to filmmaking with a background in dance, still photography, and editing. She not only directs films that address the African-American experience, but she has also been actively involved in the promotion and distribution of hundreds of black films as the program director of the Black Filmmakers Foundation (1981–84) and as an activist and lecturer. She is a multitalented individual who is an inspiration to many others. Ayoka Chenzira, along with a number of other Black women filmmakers, is clearly forging an entirely new kind of cinema. She has said that she is more inspired by Toni Morrison than by any filmmakers. She is equally inspired by her daughter and her husband, Thomas Pinnock, a choreographer. Chenzira studied at NYU Film School.

Hair Piece: A Film for Nappy-Headed People (1982) is an animated film that explores the politics of African-American female identity through an analysis of hair and hair styling. Chenzira's satire of black hair-care products, devices, and attitudes toward hair in black culture is one of a new genre of black documentaries that studies cultural history in a fresh manner. Like Black British filmmaker Maureen Blackwood's *Perfect Image?* (1988), Julie Dash's *Illusions* (1983), and Kathleen Collins' *Losing Ground, Hair Piece* is one of a growing body of films whose images are situated within a contextual exploration of Black women's multifaceted cultural identity.

Ayoka Chenzira's *Secret Sounds Screaming: The Sexual Abuse of Children* (1982) is a video documentary on sexual abuse from an Afrocentric point of view. Chenzira's approach to the material is novel. In the film, Chenzira blends the voices of experiences of people of color, for the first time addressing the issue from a nonwhite perspective. Chenzira's film differs from many other films that deal with child sexual abuse because of her ability to uncover the societal support system that allows and in some ways encourages the sexual abuse of children. Chenzira couples these criticisms with an examination of the laws that allow sex offenders to go free, and the attitudes that promote a power-relationship that encourages and promotes sexual child abuse.

Chenzira's film *Syvilla* (1979) is a celebration of dance in African-American history, as is her subsequent work *Zajota and the Boogie Spirit* (1989). Chenzira is annoyed when she is called "the female Spike Lee." She is particularly aware of the particularities of Black women's filmmaking. As she told Greg Tate:

> A lot of the Black men directors who are popular now I've known for years. Back when they were lobbying for Black film like I was, before they decided to go to Hollywood and said fuck it. I've seen articles written by men and women about the "new black cinema" and no one seems to ask, where are the women? Because it's so obviously missing you just tend to go, hello, hello? Obviously, and I underline obviously, the women are missing from the arena and the men tend to act as if the women don't exist. . . . I really don't intend to sound either overly romantic or cosmic or ethereal, but to me it's real simple: I'm a person here on the planet who's here working out some stuff. I come to film thinking of it as an art form. My work comes from a very private place. It doesn't come from marketing statistics. (1991, 78)

Gurinder Chadha

Border crossings and diaspora are at the center of Kenya-born, Punjabi-parented Asian/African filmmaker Gurinder Chadha. Raised in London, Chadha became interested in film when she wrote a dissertation on Indian women in British cinema. Among her early projects is a video entitled *Pain, Passion and Profit* (1992). In this documentary, Chadha shows how several African women successfully develop small businesses, and the impact that their success has on the community and the economic development of women. *Pain, Passion and Profit* evokes a spiritual connection between women in the "First" and "Third" worlds. In 1989, Chadha made a documentary film entitled *I'm British but . . .* that has been championed as a postmodern performative documentary. In the film, Chadha intercuts interviews of assimilated British Pakistanis who now call themselves unhyphenated Scots, Welsh, and English with a shot of a Bangla music group. As Bill Nichols argues, the music "reminds us of the colonial legacy and its racist continuation that cannot be so readily erased" (96).

Bhaji on the Beach (1994) is Gurinder Chadha's first feature film. Written by Meera Syal, *Bhaji at the Beach* is a metanarrative of difference, a complex, yet witty look at nine Asian women, spanning three generations. Like the third-generation Asian immigrants in *I'm British but . . .*, the women in *Bhaji* tell one another's secrets. As Chadha explained to Ann Hornaday of the *New York Times*, "*Bhaji* is also about subverting many expectations of women" (29). Financed by Channel 4, *Bhaji on the Beach* is set at a seaside resort in Blackpool. Simi, played by Shaheen Khan, organizes the all-girl trip, announcing, "it's not often we women get away from the demands of patriarchy . . . struggling as we do between the double yoke of racism and sexism. . . . Have a female fun time!" As the day unfolds, the complexities of race and gender become more pronounced.

Chadha's film cuts across lines of difference, yet it is not so conventional as to erase cultural differences. "The idea of making a film about Asian women that ordinary Asian women from where I grew up would be able to see and enjoy was important," Chadha told Lawrence Chua, of the *Village Voice* (62). *Bhaji* was produced by Nadine Marsh-Edwards, a founding member of the Black British filmmaking cooperative, Sankofa Films. Chadha is currently at work on her next film project, which centers on lives of Asians from Kenya, who, like Chadha, have relocated in England. In all her works, Gurinder Chadha is creating a New Black British cinema of diaspora that deftly combines education with pure entertainment.

Camille Billops

African-American filmmaker Camille Billops is well known in feminist and Black diasporic circles for her autobiographical filmmaking that actively resists the dominant ways of looking, knowing, and embodying Black female subjectivity. In 1987, Billops codirected (with James Hatch) a documentary entitled *Older Women and Love* that mixed strategies of objectivity and subjectivity into a personal statement of Black female subjectivity. Mixing dramatizations, and on-camera interviews, Billops and Hatch discovered the pains and pleasures of intergenerational relationships. The film was based on Billops' eighty-year-old mother who, Billops discovered, was having a wonderful sex life with a man half her age. As Barbara Lekatsas writes in the *Third World Newsreel Catalogue, Older Women and Love*: "Dispels myths about the type of sexual life older women enjoy . . . focusing on strong women who battle to get their way and who also pay the price by taking risks, the film shows the realistic challenges of independence" (16).

In their next film, *Suzanne, Suzanne* (1982), Camille Billops and James Hatch mixed hybrid styles of documentary "subjectivity" and "objectivity" in a study of familial abuse cycles. In this unique and ground-breaking film, Suzanne, a young African-American woman, confronts the legacies of a family life of domestic abuse. *Suzanne, Suzanne* was also semiautobiographical. In this case, the film was based on Billops' niece, Suzanne, who kicked a heroin habit after confronting her abusive father. Suzanne faces her drug abuse problem af-

ter confronting her abusive father and complicitous mother about the domestic abuse she suffered as a young girl. After many years of silence, Suzanne is
finally able to confront her mother's pain and the complexities of a household
situation of domestic abuse. Billops' extraordinarily honest and moving portrayal of Suzanne's growing subjectivity and reclamation of her body and her
history is without comparison. *Suzanne, Suzanne* directly confronts the facade
of middle-class decorum that often serves to suppress knowledge of domestic
abuse situations.

In 1991, Camille Billops and James Hatch directed *Finding Christa*, another
documentary of self-knowledge, this time about Billops herself and her reun-
ion with her own daughter whom she gave up for adoption twenty years prior
to the film. *Finding Christa* was an considerable critical success, probably due
to its unflinching honesty and its hybrid documentary style. As Billops told
Lynda Jones of the *Village Voice*, Billops left her child at the Children's Home
Society in California, in order to pursue her goals as an artist:

> I just knew I didn't want to be a mother, I wasn't good at it. That this was a
> feminist statement is hindsight. Everyone had a problem with it. Men leave,
> but women are supposed to endure Fatherless houses? Unwed mothers? Is that
> something attractive? I didn't think so. So I reversed it. They say you don't have
> a lot of choices, but you do. You just have to have the courage to take them. . . .
> They would ask me why I don't cry. And I asked them what a 30-year-old tear
> would look like. If I had been a victim, a drug addict, or a prostitute, they
> would have forgiven me. But go off to be an artist, be happy, running off with
> a white male? (60)

Billops is uncompromising in her Black activist feminism. She and her husband James Hatch have also been active as black archivists, opening the Hatch-
Billops Collection of African-American History in Soho. The archive includes
thousands of oral histories of African-American artists in dance, theatre, and
film. Billops became an artist and filmmaker after graduating with an MFA
from City College of New York in 1973. She explains that her creativity could
not be held back by racism in art and film communities, and in society. She
told Jones, "You have to have a certain sense of defiance in you so you don't
self-destruct. They can't stop the creative thing in you" (60).

Billops' films are in a way self-expressions of Black female subjectivity. They
also are exorcisms in a way, or film therapy. Billops' most recent film, *The KKK
Boutique Ain't Just Rednecks* (1994), directly confronts racism in the context
of "political correctness." This film is a direct refutation that "PC" culture is

changing racism. Instead, the film exposes how racism is developing in new forms and locations. As Billops explains:

> The secret in finding out about racism is exploring your own and once that's done, we can ask what racism means. And who benefits. People that have power don't want to give it up. White women aren't going to give it to black women. And white men aren't going to give it to black men. I think we've come up with some good answers in this film. (Jones 60)

Camille Billops exemplifies a decolonizing oppositional film gaze, as described by bell hooks in *Black Looks*: "Indeed, a fundamental task of black critical thinkers has been the struggle to break with hegemonic codes of seeing, thinking, and being that block our capacity to see ourselves oppositionally, to imagine, describe, and invent ourselves in ways that are liberatory" (2).

Billops continues to make independent films that are challenging and personal as much as they are uncompromising. Despite funding obstacles, she supports her filmmaking with private donations, sales of her artwork, and a network of family members who support her artwork. Her most recent film, *String of Pearls*, returns to her family for another autobiographical documentary, this time concentrating on her stepfather. Why does she make personal films? "It's like leaving pebbles in the sand, a need to prove we were here" (Jones, 60).

Barbara McCullough

Los Angeles-based filmmaker Barbara McCullough is an African-American director whose films celebrate the African diaspora. McCullough's films go beyond resisting spectatorship and create "a space for the assertion of a critical black female spectatorship . . . they do not simply offer diverse representations, they imagine new transgressive possibilities for the formulation of identity," as bell hooks describes the new Afrocentric film tradition (1992, 130). McCullough became interested in filmmaking after an artistic career in photography, and told writer Elizabeth Jackson that she was inspired by the example of Zora Neale Hurston (94–97). Stylistically, McCullough's films nod to Hurston's influence. McCullough directly confronts white critical disparagement of African womanist artists, especially in *Shopping Bag Spirits* (1980). In the film, McCullough explores the place of ritual in African-American life. Clyde Taylor finds that it is Black women filmmakers who tend to invoke African sources as "vehicles of symbol, icon, and ritual" (1986, 29). *Shopping Bag Spirits* is a ritualistic display of repetitive catharsis, which features the work of the diasporic community. McCullough's earlier film, *Water Ritual #1* (1970), also evokes an Afrocentric cultural past through the use of ritual. In the short film, an African woman refigures the deteriorating urban environment with a female fertility statue. In a purification ritual, the woman begins to reclaim her environment, her body, and her soul.

In her interview with Elizabeth Jackson, McCullough explains some of the difficulties she finds as an independent African-American director: "Whites are still doing the hiring. . . . In what I do [working with special visual effects] there are only a very few black people out there. I have been the only one whom I have come across in a management position in this area" (96). McCullough observes that it is incredibly difficult to access equipment, find funding, and obtain widespread distribution. Nevertheless, McCullough holds out hope for aspiring Black independents. "Resilience is the key to surviving in the midst of all of this" (Jackson 97). McCullough's Black feminist cultural ideological perspective infuses her avant-garde films "as participating art suggesting a paradigm for personal and collective introspection" (Gibson 377). McCullough is an admirer of the films of Julie Dash. Both share a uniqueness and authenticity that suggests that Black women filmmakers find multiple approaches to similar, though individualized, themes.

Barbara McCullough's *World Saxophone Quartet* (1980) is an internationally well-known short film that features the jazz quartet of the same name. Though McCullough could not convince any PBS affiliate to run her more formalist works, they did accept and feature *World Saxophone Quartet* in 1988. McCullough's films have developed a reputation through word of mouth, and they are shown at international film festivals, particularly during Black History Month. McCullough has worked extensively in commercial production as a production manager, unit production manager, and a visual effects artist at Ciné Motion Pictures. She currently works in computer animation and digital special effects.

Alile Sharon Larkin

Born May 6, 1953, Alile Sharon Larkin grew up in Pasadena, California. Larkin studied creative writing as an undergraduate at the University of Southern California. Larkin earned an MFA in Film and Television Production from UCLA. As cofounder of the Black Filmmakers Collective, Alile Sharon Larkin is a leading Black filmmaker, educator, activist, and writer. Larkin has been active as a filmmaker since 1979. In addition to her directorial achievements, Larkin is also an advocate of children's educational television. In 1984,

Larkin directed the cable production *My Dream Is to Marry An African Prince* (1984). In 1989, Larkin formed NAP Productions, which produces films and videos for African-American children. Alile Sharon Larkin's best known film is *A Different Image* (1982). In the film, a young woman named Alana, played by Margot Saxton-Federella, attempts to escape the stereotypical defining powers of race and gender. As Alana looks at images of African women, she wonders where she fits into her own culture. Her boyfriend Vincent misunderstands Alana's quest for self-representation and identity. Alana tells him, "You just have to see me differently. You have to learn to respect me."

In her article "Black Women Filmmakers Defining Ourselves: Feminism in Our Own Voice," Larkin comments that *A Different Image* received mostly positive criticism but "some negative criticism has come from 'radical' feminists and Marxists . . . it would be their demand that I condemn black men and align myself with white women against patriarchy" (171). Larkin points out that "feminism succumbs to racism when it segregates black women from black men and dismisses our history. The assumption that black women and white women share identical or similar histories and experiences presents an important problem. . . . Feminism must address these issues, otherwise its ahistorical approach towards black women can and does maintain institutional racism" (158–59). In *A Different Image*, Larkin explores multiple perspectives on the problems of racism and sexism in African-American culture. She gathered images from a variety of different sources, using both stock footage and original photography, finding the money for the film as she went along. Larkin's philosophy toward low budget filmmaking is accurately described in her comments: "There seem to be two schools among independents. Wait until you have all the money, or shoot what you can when you can. I shoot what I can when I can" (Acker 131).

Maureen Blackwood

Black British filmmaker Maureen Blackwood is a founding member of Sankofa, a London-based collective dedicated to promoting and producing Black films by Black directors. In 1983, Martina Attile, Maureen Blackwood, Robert Crusz, Isaac Julien, and Nadine Marsh-Edwards formed the group to explore diverse images of the Black experience beyond the realms of the exotic, the victim, and the violent assailant. In 1986, Maureen Blackwood and Isaac Julien directed *The Passion of Remembrance* for Sankofa. *The Passion of Remembrance* is considered a unique representation of the diversity of the experience of Black people. The multi-leveled narrative is an experiment in multiple point of view. In the film, a Black couple talk about the subject of diversity in Black experience in a self-referential act of cinematic framing and doubling. The reconfiguration of Black identity is grounded within the context of a series of rapidly changing video images of British history.

Perfect Image? (1988) is an exploration of the notion of self and identity, seen through the perspective of two women, one dark skinned and one light. The actresses reach across the screen and draw the viewer into an intimate experience through their disregard for the camera apparatus. In this way, Blackwood moves the discourse to a subjective level, guiding the viewer on a rediscovery of her or his notion of self. Stereotypes of Black women are thrown into a fresh perspective in this film. As Barbara Kruger observes, the films of the Sankofa collective "break down the conventions of what is 'appropriate' Black visual production" (144). Blackwood's films are a movement toward an openly defined counter-cinema of black expression.

In 1992, Blackwood directed a documentary film about the unsung contributions of Black Britons in boxing and music halls at the turn of the century. *A Family Called Abrew* (1992) is a warm and poignant browse through archival footage, oral history, and other important documentation of the neglected cultural moment in Black history. The film concentrates on one particularly extraordinary family, the Abrews. As cultural and historical documents of lost family and racial identity, films such as *A Family Called Abrew* mark the rebirth of Black cinema.

Home Away from Home is a short film about a Black woman named Miriam. Miriam lives near Heathrow Airport. Blackwood uses the metaphor of the continual mobility of the planes in the air over Miriam's house to underscore Miriam's displacement from her African cultural roots. Miriam wishes to reconnect with her exiled home, in order to share her earth-mother home-place with her daughter, Fumi. She builds a mud hut in her garden and creates a mystical space in which she metaphorically escapes her exiled existence. *Home Away from Home* is a meditation on exile and spiritual communion. In addition to directing, Maureen Blackwood is constantly active in all phases of production on other Sankofa films. She is a formidable figure in Black filmmaking in Britain and an admired feminist and a role model abroad.

Martina Attile

A member of the Black filmmaking collective Sankofa, Martina Attile directed *Dreaming Rivers* in 1988. The thirty-minute film is comparable to Julie

Dash's epic *Daughters of the Dust* in that both tell the tale of Caribbean families that experience migration. Both films are connected by the theme of exile and the importance of community and the physical landscape. In *Dreaming Rivers*, however, the narrative revolves around an older woman, "Miss T.," who has been left in her one-room apartment by her husband and children who have been drawn away to pursue their dreams. The title refers to the fragmentary nature of the memories of the family, who gather together for Miss T.'s funeral after her death. The film is richly metaphorical and allegorical, and an important entry in the developing canon of new Black filmmaking.

In the spring of 1984, the Black Women and Representation Workshops were formed in London and funded by the Greater London Arts Council. The film workshops are led by such filmmaker/critics as Martina Attile and Maureen Blackwood. The workshops discuss such topics as Black stereotypes, the control of images, access to control of images, and often include screenings as well as formal and informal workshops. In the notes from the workshop of 1984, Attile and Blackwood explain that their goal is to "establish an ongoing forum for discussion around the social and political implications of the fragmentation of Black women in film/video/television" (203). Among the activities of the workshop are screenings and discussions of the "mammy" figure in such Hollywood films as *Gone With the Wind*, *Imitation of Life*, and popular cartoons from the thirties and forties.

Sankofa workshop participants discuss the colonialist depiction of the Black female body as a "dark continent" that is colonized by mainstream Hollywood cinema. The ability to re-look at painfully racist images is an important step towards defining ownership of Black female identity. The efforts of Sankofa, the Black Women and Representation Workshops, Women in Sync, and the Black Audio Collective represent enormous steps toward a counter-cinema of black female ownership. The Sankofa style is a move away from linear narrative filmmaking toward a montagist approach of multilayeredness that embraces the multivalencies of everyday experience. Martina Attile is to be credited for her input into the development of the Sankofa collective as well as for her activism and filmmaking.

Dawn Suggs

New Yorker Dawn Suggs credits Camille Billops as a strong influence in her filmmaking career. Suggs, an African-American lesbian avant-garde director explores lesbian sexuality and the silences around sexuality in her pioneering short films. *Chasing the Moon* (1991) is Suggs' stark black and white vision of an assault on a Black lesbian woman. The short film is cathartic in the way that Billops' films are. Suggs told Greg Tate that hers is a personal cinema that bespeaks silences:

> I felt it would be cathartic to put feelings of alienation and desire-anxiety on film. It was a response to so many women I'd met who'd had devastating, traumatic experiences in their lives, a lot of times from sexual abuse, and were seeking to escape in every way imaginable—drugs, strange relationships. It's not a literal film. I just wanted to speak to that pain. We need to see more work about Black lesbians and their world. I'm editing a film about a lesbian couple where one woman wants to have a baby, doesn't want artificial insemination, but through having sex with an old male friend, so that's the conflict. Another script plays with this idea of lesbians as wild sexual freaks. Silence is one of our languages too. Silence can be used in a very empowering way. Through your marginality you find different types of tools. In time our silence can be used very effectively. (1991, 77)

In *I Never Danced the Way Girls Were Supposed To* (1992) Suggs combines film and video in a cinematic poem that meditates and mediates Black lesbian subjectivity and sexuality. Dawn Suggs continues to make distinctively personal films that recover and discover Black lesbian female subjectivity.

Cheryl Dunye

Another Black lesbian cineaste, Cheryl Dunye began making autobiographical treatments in 1990 with *Janine. Janine* is a sometimes painful autoethnography of Dunye's relationship with a high school friend, Janine, an upper-class white woman. Dunye talks directly to the viewer, telling us how she desired to be part of Janine's cultural milieu, despite many obstacles. Writing in the *Village Voice*, critic Amy Taubin commented that "Cheryl Dunye's autobiographical *Janine* combines a no-frills talking-head image with remarkable writing (as qtd. in *Third World Newsreel* 20). The film is comparable to Yvonne Welbon's *Sisters In the Life: First Love* (1993), another example of Black lesbian autobiographical filmmaking in the 1970s, and also the films of Dawn Suggs.

Dunye's next film, *She Don't Fade* (1991), is a black and white video that tells the story of a Black lesbian named Shae Clarke, played by Dunye herself. The film is a quest for a lover, in which Dunye's portrayal of Shae Clarke is both poignant and powerful. Cindy Fuchs, writing in the *City Paper*, called the video "a lively lesbian love story, which integrates the details of video-making into the story itself: it's sharp, funny, and intelligent" (qtd. in *Third World Newsreel*

20). The video was screened at the Women in the Director's Chair Festival, the New Festival, and was given numerous other international film and video screenings. In *The Potluck and the Passion* (1993), which was honored by a screening at the Whitney Museum of American Art Biennial in the year of its production, Cheryl Dunye again focuses on lesbian relationships and lesbian subjectivity in another auto-ethnographic poem. This time the setting is an anniversary party. The film is noted for its combination of humor, articulation of desire, and personal/public politics.

Christine Choy

Christine Choy is a major figure in the Asian-American disaporic cinema. Choy was born in China to a Chinese mother and a Korean father. Her father left her family in 1953 to return to his home in Korea. Choy was raised by her mother, who became independent out of necessity. After the cultural revolution in China, Choy and her mother returned to Korea and were reunited with her father. She developed a taste for American films in Korea, but she couldn't help notice that Asian people were treated as second-class citizens in American films. Choy's films reflect her experiences and her politics. As a director who is familiar with the struggles of exile and migration and she infuses her autobiographical experiences into her films, such as *Spikes and Spindles* (1976). The film concerns Chinese migration, exile, and cultural identity politics. The labels of identity are a central preoccupation of Choy, who is herself classified as a "political filmmaker," an "immigrant," an "Asian," a "woman of color," and as she says, "the list goes on and on and on" (Hanson 17).

Choy's *Who Killed Vincent Chin?* (1988) is, in its own way, an examination of racist labels and their lethal ramifications. Codirected with Renee Tajima, *Who Killed Vincent Chin?* was nominated for an Academy Award for Best Documentary. It is based on a true story of a murder in Detroit in 1982 of a Chinese man by white men who were subsequently fined $3,000 and punished with only three years' probation. Choy made the film despite difficulties securing funding from the Corporation for Public Broadcasting. Choy managed to see the project through, raising $175,000 from CPB and another $95,000 from other sources. Finally, the film was screened by PBS as part of the series "Point of View." Choy situates the murder contextually within the anti-Asian sentiment brewing in America as a result of the economic growth of Japan and the economic fall of the United States. Intercut with the actual story of the murder are clips of closed American car factories, ads for Chryslers, and newsreel footage of Asian-American history. Choy and Tajima examine the complexities of attitudes that contributed to the murder, from the xenophobic attitude toward foreign cars to the racism against any nonwhite peoples. *Who Killed Vincent Chin?* is a strong multicultural American film that reconfigures ethnographic filmmaking.

Ann Hui

Born in Manchuria, China, Ann Hui is an important figure of the Hong Kong New Wave cinema. Hui became a director after earning a master's degree in English and comparative literature. She spent two years studying at the London Film School and returned to Hong Kong in 1975 where she immediately began directing television documentaries and narrative films. *The Boy From Vietnam* (1978), *The Story of Woo Viet* (1981), and *Boat People* (1983) form a trilogy of films centering on the problems of Vietnamese and Chinese refugees. Hui has a talent for using Western genres as set pieces for social commentary. *The Story of Woo Viet* borrows from the gangster film to tell the story of a Chinese man from Vietnam who escapes to Hong Kong. Hoping to escape to America, the man is forced by circumstance into exile at sea, a fate all too common for Vietnamese refugees.

Hui's *Boat People* was internationally recognized at the Cannes Film Festival and received international distribution. *Boat People* raised a great deal of controversy because of Hui's handling of the issue of Vietnamese refugees in the film and because of its political stance. Some viewers found the film excessively violent. Karen Jaehne asked Hui if the torture scenes were necessary, to which Hui responded, "No, the violence was in fact restrained. When I showed it to some of the refugees I knew, they asked me—why had I not shown some of the [more] dreadful violence" (17). *Boat People* was banned in China. In *Hong Kong*, as Li Cheuk-to writes, the film "touched a collective nerve among Hong Kong people who were by now increasingly worried over their future" (167).

Ann Hui is one of several Hong Kong New Wave directors who are forging a hybrid style of cinema that bridges cultural differences, their work falling somewhere between tradition and Westernization. Hui's recent film *The Song of the Exile* (1990) is a semiautobiographical tale of a Hong Kong woman who returns from London to Hong Kong for her sister's wedding. The cultural differences among the mother, daughter, and sister cause conflict between the three women figures. *The Song of the Exile* also shows the effects of racial discrimination. The protagonist is faced with job discrimination in England, cultural differences with her family in Hong Kong, and the cultural isolation of identity politics.

Merata Mita

Merata Mita is the first Maori woman to ever direct a feature film (*Mauri*, 1988). Born in 1942 at Maketu, Mita is of the Ngati Pikiao tribe. She grew up in a traditional Maori household and remains tied to her cultural upbringing. Mita found herself drawn into the film trade because of her ability to translate for European film crews who hired her to work as a cultural guide on their films about the Maori people. She decided that ethnographic films about her people should be directed by Maori people. Mita is well versed in the politics of objectification of the other, the cultural colonialization of indigenous peoples by non indigenous filmmakers. Consequently, Mita's films are not simple documentaries on Maori issues, but they are studies on the presumed objectivity of the ethnographic traditional cinema.

In *Patu!* (1984) Mita revisions documentary as an embrace of subjectivity. Mita dispenses with the notion of the "objective" filmmaker and foregrounds her own subjective position. *Patu!* is a post colonial study across Maori and South African cultural suppression. Mita uses a polylogue of voices of indigenous peoples on the soundtrack of *Patu!*, along with music designed to underscore Mita's outrage about the treatment of Maori people. Merata Mita's approach to documentary is in some ways comparable to the subjective documentary work of Vietnamese-born Trinh T. Minh-ha. Both filmmakers scrutinize the voyeuristic, objectifying gaze of the ethnographic filmmaker, and both call attention to themselves as active participants in the filmmaking process. The appropriation of the images of colonized peoples is directly bound up with the appropriation of the land and culture of indigenous people.

Maori people have been a traditional subject of colonist film directors who have misconstructed Maori identity as savage "Other." Maori directors such as Merata Mita are taking back ownership of their own images by producing Maori-language television programs, feature films, and documentaries. Their work has not always met with respect or approval from white audiences and legislators. *Patu!*, for example, was at the center of controversy when New Zealanders were outraged that the film was financed by government subsidies. The release of the film was delayed for several years because of the controversy. *Mauri* (1988) caused considerably fewer problems with the public. The film centers around a strong grandmother figure who realizes the significance of spiritual loss in Maori women who are deculturated into the dominant Pakeha culture of New Zealand. Mita is concerned with the loss of oral culture, ritual meaning, and Maori identity.

Tracey Moffatt

Australian Black filmmaker Tracey Moffatt makes films that challenge dominant myths about Aboriginal people. Aboriginal people are represented in mainstream films as either absent, "uncivilized," or happily colonized, while Australians are depicted as cultural heroes. While it is true that "the cultural image of Australia is not a monolithic mythic image" (Rattigan 24), Aboriginal experiences are typically denarrated or viewed through a colonialist perspective. *A Change of Face* (1988) is a documentary about colonialist cultural image-making. Moffatt interviews media professionals—actors, directors, and producers—and captures their racism and sexism in their on- camera responses. Moffatt's othering of the colonizer is a decolonizing technique, designed to demythologize the power of powerful representatives of the media. Trinh T. Minh-ha characterizes such a displacing and decentering design as an instance of "she who steals language" (1989, 15). Moffatt steals the cinematic language of the oppressor and uses that same language to revision history and rearticulate the location of Aboriginal people.

Moffatt's *Nice Colored Girls* (1987) continues on the trajectory of demythologizing and revising Australian historicity. *Nice Colored Girls* exposes the history of exploitation of Aboriginal women by white men. Moffatt interweaves extradiegetic sounds, images, and printed texts to convey the multiple perspectives of Aboriginal women. *Nice Colored Girls*, however, is not an ahistorical reconstruction of Aboriginal women, as Moffatt acknowledges the role of oppression and enforced silence in the construction of colonized Aboriginal women. This identification of the subaltern is juxtaposed against a recognition of the acculturated modern urban Aboriginal woman in an unusual counternarrative. Thus Moffatt escapes the tendency to represent the Aboriginal woman as a monolithic subject.

Night Cries (1990) exposes the problematic relationships between women across cultural margins. In the film, a middle-aged Aboriginal woman nurses her adopted white mother, and the psychology of racism between the two women involves both love and hostility. *Night Cries* is an exploration and indictment of assimilation policies that once forced Aboriginal children to be raised by white families, in which Moffatt utilizes expressionistic sets that serve to underscore the allegorical nature of the film as a fictive, staged construct. As a storyteller, Tracey Moffatt uses formalist strategies to revision history and incorporate Aboriginal histories into contemporary filmmaking. Like the recent Renaissance of storytelling by Australian Aboriginal women documented by Kateryna Olijnyk Longley (370–84), Tracey Moffat's work is a testament to a living culture that refuses to be subsumed into the dominant Australian society. Tracey Moffatt's reclamation of black Australian feminine subjectivity is thus a truly important and essential cultural project.

Maria Novaro

Maria Novaro is viewed as one of the most outstanding women filmmakers in Mexico and she is proud of her feminist cinematic vision. In an interview following the release of her film *Danzón* (1992), Novaro said that "I like it very much when people come away thinking 'only a woman could have made that film' " (Golden 24). *Danzón*, which stars Maria Rojo and Daniel Rergis, builds a feminist narrative from a plot line that seems at once to combine neorealism and melodrama. The film concerns the life of Julia (Maria Rojo), a dancer and a telephone operator, who goes in search of her missing dance partner. Stylistically, Julia's story unfolds in the tradition of neorealism, as Novaro's camera flatly records Mexico City dance hall culture. Novaro frequented these dance halls and became fascinated by their cultural significance. The dances themselves signify a fairy tale narrative of romantic perfection, yet the dancers' lives are marked by brutal hard work, uncompromising physical perfection, and competition. Julia's search for her missing dance partner, however, seems destined to conclude in a traditional Mexican melodramatic narrative ending. The viewer is carried along by a desire for the expected archetypal ending of the romantic melodrama: the reuniting of the heterosexual couple. Though Julia is one of the finest, most well recognized dancers, she loses her status when she loses her partner. Thus, as Gabriel Garcia Marquez argues, Novaro "is trying to reveal something about the condition of women in Mexico" (Golden 24).

Danzón refigures female subjectivity through its hybridization of melodramatic expectation and neorealist staging. Moreover, Julia does not conform to the traditional configuration of women in Mexican melodrama. She is neither the "archetypal good mother," nor the "*mala mujer* [bad woman]," identified by Ana M. López in her study of the Mexican melodrama (261). Julia's partner (Daniel Rergis) turns out to be an elegant older man, not the dashing young romantic hero whom we expect to literally sweep Julia off her feet. Julia defines herself through her search, which ends with a recognition of self, rather than a usurpation of female as object.

Danzón was highly successful on an international level. It was the first Mexican film to be invited to the Directors' Fortnight at the Cannes Film Festival. Some critics compared the film unfavorably with Novaro's subsequent release, *Lola* (1988–1989), a film noted for its gritty social realism. A narrative of the plight of a single mother, *Lola* exposes urban decay and miserable living conditions of the areas at the outskirts of Mexico City. Both *Danzón* and *Lola* were cowritten by Novaro and her younger sister, Beatriz Novaro. Maria Novaro's films show a consistent interest in social issues and female fantasy, desire, and need. In 1982, Novaro directed *Conmigo las pararas muy bien*, a film in which a woman uses magic to make her nagging husband and child disappear, while in *Querida Carmen* (1983), a woman imagines herself as a liberated cowgirl. These early Novaro efforts display her ludic approach to female desire and subjectivity. Novaro's films challenge traditional notions of female identity in which "she can be either the wife *or* the sexual object" (López 267). More recently, Novaro directed *El Jardin del Edén* (*The Garden of Eden*) in 1994.

Alanis Obomsawin

Alanis Obomsawin is a Canadian-based Native American filmmaker. Obomsawin is one of a growing number of independent Native-American filmmakers and video artists including Sandra Sunrising Osawa, Susan Fanshel, Arlene Bowman, and Mona Smith. Obomsawin grew up on an Abenaki reserve near Montreal, and later made a career for herself as a singer, becoming nationally famous. Obomsawin was subsequently asked to act as consultant on several film projects for the National Film Board of Canada. Eventually, Obomsawin began work on her own films. Her first projects were children's films, such as *Christmas at Moose Factory* (1971), in which she utilized children's artwork as source material.

Obomsawin's films demonstrate a consistent need to document the cultural traditions of Abenaki and other Native American peoples. *Mother of Many Children* (1977) documents the everyday lives and customs of Native American women from a cross-cultural perspective. Obomsawin traveled across Canada to document their lives on film. In general, women's rituals, both Native American and non-Native American, "have been largely ignored by folklorists, ethnographers, and literary [and film] critics," as Paula Gunn Allen concludes (268). The paucity of scholarship on Native American filmmaking, and particularly Native women's filmmaking, characterizes an acceptance of the myth that Native Americans have made no films. The continual devaluation and lack of distribution of Native American women's films helps to support the myth.

Alanis Obomsawin continues to make films despite the suppression of Native American women's voices. In 1986, Obomsawin directed *Cardinal: Cry from a Diary of a Métis Child.* This film documents the life of a young orphaned child who is shuffled from one foster home to another and finally commits suicide. Obomsawin continually tackles political issues, such as the governmental invasion of the Micmac reserve, in *Incident at Restigouche* (1984). Her latest film, *Poundmaker's Lodge: A Healing Place* (1987), is about Native Americans and alcoholism. The film documents a program that works to cure alcoholism by returning to Native customs and rituals and observes the issues of insider-outsider status of assimilated Native Americans. *Poundmaker's Lodge* provides a glimpse into the complexities around the issues of Native identity and celebrates Native cosmology and subjectivity.

Sarah Maldoror

Sarah Maldoror is probably one of the best known African women directors of a growing number of African filmmakers. Maldoror told Sylvia Harvey that she dislikes categorization by nationality: "I'm against all forms of nationalism. Nationalities and borders between countries have to disappear. . . . I have to live where the money is to be raised, and then do my work in Africa" (75). Maldoror transcends the Eurocentric category of Third World woman director. As Chandra Mohanty writes, such categorization "is a mode of appropriation and codification" (1984, 337), which denies African women political consciousness and agency.

Sarah Maldoror is a political filmmaker whose perspective comes out of a commitment to political agency and postcolonial consciousness. Though she is best known to the Western world for *Sambizanga* (1972), a political call for action, Maldoror has had quite an extraordinary career as film director and political activist. Mario de Andrade, a noted Angolan political activist, writer, and leader of the Angolan liberation movement, is married to Sarah Maldoror. Maldoror studied at the Moscow Film Academy and became politically active in the 1950s. She was involved in the African liberation movement in France, and she also founded the theatre group "Les Griotes," an agitprop collective, for which Maldoror adapted works by Jean-Paul Sartre and other political writers for the stage. Before she became a film director, Maldoror worked as Gillo Pontecorvo's collaborator on *The Battle of Algiers* (1966). The classic neorealist film records the blood bath between Algerian freedom fighters and French militia in 1957 and 1958.

Over many years, Maldoror has worked in African cinema as a political activist against colonialism and postcolonial rule. *Sambizanga* (1972) depicts a central female revolutionary in Angola. As Manthia Diawara argues, *Sambizanga* has been unfairly "criticized for being 'too beautiful' and therefore less authentic to African realities." These critics of the film ignore Maldoror's intent, according to Diawara, "to create a positive role for women in the revolution" (1992, 90). *Sambizanga* exemplifies a third cinema "able to challenge official versions of history" (Gabriel 1989, 57). The film reinscribes the role of women in revolutionary politics. As Maldoror told Sylvia Harvey, her feminist agenda went beyond representational imagery:

> I'm only interested in women who struggle. These are the women I want to have in my films, not the others. I also offer work to as many women as possible during the time I'm shooting my films. You have to support those women who want to work with film. Up until now, we are still few in number, but if you support those women in film who are around, then slowly our numbers will grow. (75)

Sambizanga won awards at many international film festivals. The film is screened regularly in African film festivals, women's film festivals, and African and women's studies courses. Sarah Maldoror is an activist for African cinema who sees the role of political marginalization of African film as part of a larger context of colonial imperialism.

Safi Faye

One of a growing number of independent African-born women directors, Safi Faye was born in Dakar. Faye is of Serer origin. The Serer people live in Senegal and have a strong cultural heritage, which Safi Faye records in *Fad'jal* (1979). Fad'jal is the village where Safi Faye's parents were born. Faye received her teaching certificate in 1963 and began teaching in the Dakar school system. Though she has traveled and studied abroad, Faye maintains close ties with her family and cultural roots. Faye studied ethnology at the Ecole Pratique des Hautes Etudes and the Louis Lumière Film School in the 1970s. She worked in film sound effects, as an actor, and as a model to support her studies. After gaining experience as a student filmmaker, Safi Faye began looking for financial backing to shoot a feature film.

Faye found support from the French Ministry of Cooperation and made *Kaddu Beykat* [News from my village] in 1975. The film is a semiautobiographical work, a fictionalized study of a village that suffers economically because its people refuse to go along with a colonial demand for single-crop cultivation. *Kaddu Beykat* was shot on a shoestring budget with a crew of three, according to Françoise Pfaff. Safi Faye's approach to filmmaking departs from Eurocentric documentary techniques that regard African peoples as the "other" or the cultural object. Faye's film is meant for an African audience. As Faye told Angela Martin in an interview at Cannes, her films are not "the observations of a stranger—a Westerner. . . . I give people a voice, and I take a position within that" (18). Faye explains that she acts as an observer-participant, and she sees film as a form of community expression. For example, for *Kaddu Beykat* she often took the advice of the villagers on what to film and what not to film.

Kaddu Beykat won many international prizes, including the Georges Sadoul Prize and the International Film Critics' Award at the Berlin Film Festival. It has also been screened at the Museum of Modern Art in New York, and the Racines Noires festival in Paris. Faye's ability to reconceive notions of "fiction" and "reality" challenge documentary form. As she told Angela Martin, the distinctions between fiction, documentary, and ethnology "make no sense" (18). Safi Faye's films transcend the usual documentarist representations of filmic "reality" and reinscribe the authenticity of daily village life and oral history.

In *La Passante* [The wayfarer], Faye plays an African woman living in France. A Frenchman and an African man become interested in the African woman. The film is a study of the different cultural expectations of women. *Kaddu Beykat* records the routine activities of women in fields, at home, in courtship, and in traditional healing rituals. *Les Ames du soleil* [The spirits of the sun] (1981) documents the difficult conditions which women face living in Africa in times of drought and poor health. Faye's *Selbé et tant d'autres* [Selbé and so many others] (1982) records the lives of women who are left behind in villages when men migrate to the city in search of employment opportunities. But Faye is as much interested in questions of ethnicity, identity, and emigration as she is in "women's" issues. Faye's ability to "document" as an observer-participant is important. Safi Faye is redefining African subjectivity through a Senegalese woman's point of view. Like Sarah Maldoror, Safi Faye is searching for and finding a film language that reflects African culture.

Euzhan Palcy

Born on the island of Martinique, Palcy decided to become a director at the age of ten. She told Janis Cole and Holly Dale, "I made a kind of wish. I said I have to become a filmmaker. I have to talk about my people" (158). Palcy remembers being discouraged by many people, but her father supported her artistic and political ambitions. She decided to study in France at the Rue Lumière School and at The Sorbonne. At the remarkable age of seventeen, Palcy directed *La Messagère* [The messenger] (1974) for French television. She also wrote and acted in the film. Palcy told Ally Acker that she initially met with resistance from the station manager: "The boss of the station didn't want to do it. After all, it was the first West Indian drama" (119). Palcy shot *La Messagère* on location in Martinique. Though she had little experience as a filmmaker, she made up for experience with her exuberance. "People were so excited, they worked on it for free" (Acker 119).

In Paris, Palcy continued to study and work as an assistant director for French and African films. She made another short film for French television, *The Devil's Workshop* (1981–82), and began writing and revising *Sugar Cane Alley*. *Sugar Cane Alley* was finally produced after three years of preproduction in 1983. The film is a semiautobiographical work, according to Palcy. Set in Martinique's shantytowns, *Sugar Cane Alley* is the story of a ten-year-old boy's coming of age under slavery and colonial oppression. The boy meets Mr. M., a Caribbean storyteller, who shows him the significance of oral tales and African rituals. Howard Rodman describes the film as "haunting and defiant, sentimental and astringent" (132). The film was a substantial critical hit at the Venice Film Festival. Suddenly, Palcy was being courted by Warner Brothers' executives. She told them, "If you give me a film, try to give me something that talks about black people, too, okay?" (Rodman 132).

Palcy's next film was *A Dry White Season* (1989). Financed by MGM, it was probably the first commercial film directed by a Black woman to be backed by a Hollywood studio. *A Dry White Season* drew criticism because of its focus on a white man (Donald Sutherland) as an anti-apartheid militant. Sutherland portrays a South African school teacher who is at first reluctant to believe that South African authorities beat and kill Black children. He gradually becomes an anti-apartheid activist when his gardener (Winston Ntshona) dies in police custody. Sutherland's life disintegrates as he becomes more and more involved in the anti-apartheid movement. His wife leaves him, and his daughter plots against him to assist the police. Finally Sutherland hires a lawyer (Marlon

Brando) to help him and is further assisted in his fight for justice by an African driver (Zakes Mokae). Palcy recognized the political implications of focusing on a white hero in order to garner Hollywood backing, but she dismisses her critics. "I want to scream to people who say this; they should write more, and they should join me and fight against those who have the money and the power to produce a movie" (Rodman 132).

bell hooks sees *A Dry White Season* as a call for militant resistance. hooks argues that Palcy's focus on a white man's political agitation and consciousness "is certainly a representation of whiteness that disturbs the status quo, one that challenges the white spectator to interrogate racism and liberalism in a far more progressive way than is normally seen in mainstream cinema" (1994, 360). It is not the triumph of the white hero that is the penultimate moment of the film, in fact; it is the unveiling of racism and violence against Black people that is important in the film.

Euzhan Palcy's attitude toward other women and blacks in the industry is characteristically supportive. She takes great pride that *A Dry White Season* paved the way for other Third World filmmakers. Palcy also finds it extremely encouraging that more and more women of color are making films. As for her own recent career, Palcy notes that "I didn't disappear" from filmmaking after the success of *A Dry White Season.* Palcy returned to France to direct a three-part documentary, *Aimé Cesaire: A Voice for History,* and a "fairy tale called *Simeon* . . . [h]aving just finished her long awaited screenplay for *The Bessie Coleman Saga,* Palcy is also working with Danny Glover on a Toussaint L'Ouverture project" (Devon Jackson 1996, 15).

Leslie Harris

Leslie Harris is one of the most important new African-American woman filmmakers. Born and raised in Ohio, Leslie Harris has a background in art and cinema studies. She earned an MFA in painting and moved to New York to break into the advertising business. Harris was unfulfilled in her job, and she began to write the screenplay for *Just Another Girl on the I.R.T.* (1993). Motivated by her anger at the media's predominantly negative images of being female youth, Harris wished to make a new kind of hip-hop film, a female-centered positive film.

Just Another Girl is a refreshing look at Black American urban female culture. Karen Alexander calls Harris' film "the first hip-hop film where black women are not mere sexual sideshows or threats to black manhood" (224).

Chantal, the film's protagonist, played by Ariyan Johnson, is a determined seventeen-year-old who narrates her own story. *Just Another Girl* manages to teach by example and remains entertaining by allowing Chantal matter-of-factly to tell her story. "I wanted to give people a different insight, to make a film from the perspective of a seventeen year old girl," Harris told Amy Taubin (1992, 68). Harris is a gifted storyteller with a flair for narrative technique. When Chantal speaks directly to the camera/audience, Harris disposes of the theatrical convention of the "fourth wall." After having a baby, Chantal returns to college, her boyfriend becomes an active father, and Chantal is obviously going to make her dreams come true. *Just Another Girl on the I.R.T.* is a subjective vision of Black female experience. It is equal parts realism (a gruesome birth scene) and fantasy (a happy ending). As bell hooks writes, filmmakers such as Julie Dash and Leslie Harris, "act to intervene and transform conventional filmic practices, changing notions of spectatorship . . . opening up a space for black female spectatorship. They imagine new transgressive possibilities for the formulation of identity" (1992, 130). Harris has a new screenplay, *Royalties, Rhythm and Blues*, a film about a woman hip-hop producer, which she hopes to begin shooting in the near future.

Darnell Martin

Darnell Martin's *I Like It Like That* (1994) is an international commercial and critical hit film, and one of the few major studio films by an African-American woman director (Columbia Pictures funded and distributed the project). Darnell has received a blitz of publicity, which disguises the fact that she has been working in the film industry a long time to get where she is today. Martin was born on January 7, 1964 in the Bronx. She went to college at Sarah Lawrence at the insistence of her mother, who believed that a proper education was the most important factor in determining one's later life. It was at Sarah Lawrence that Martin first got a solid glimpse of the possibilities of expressing one's own personal vision through creative work.

After graduating from Sarah Lawrence, Martin applied at several film schools but was turned down and had to take a menial job checking out rental cameras to support herself. She also appeared as an actress in the low-budget 1987 thriller *Deadly Obsession* to help pay the bills. While working at the camera rental facility, Martin made the acquaintance of Ernest Dickerson, who shot many of Spike Lee's early ground-breaking films. Impressed by Martin's spirit and tenacity, Dickerson got her a job as an assistant on Lee's *Do the Right Thing*.

By this time, Martin was beginning to attract some serious attention, and New Line Cinema offered her $2 million to film her script of *Blackout*, which would later metamorphosize into *I Like It Like That*. However, the low budget meant that the film would have to be shot very quickly, and Martin was afraid that it would compromise the quality of the finished project. Accordingly, she held out until Columbia Pictures came up with a $5.5 million budget, which would allow for nine weeks of shooting. The film began in earnest in the late summer of 1993, shooting in the Bronx. When the film was completed and screened, the press response was ecstatic.

I Like It Like That is a coming of age story, set in the mean streets of the Bronx, but told from a Latina/African-American woman's perspective. The early positive response to the film suggests that Martin has found a way to treat a woman's experience of growing up in extreme poverty, while supporting herself and her children, in a way that is simultaneously gritty and commercial. In fact, the film has been celebrated as a neorealist film of African-American/Latina Bronx culture. Darnell Martin is angry that critics jumped to the incorrect conclusion that she is the first Black woman director to be backed by a major Hollywood production company. She told Devon Jackson of the *Village Voice*, "I would rather have no one see my film than be marketed that way . . . it is an affront to the filmmakers like Julie Dash and Leslie Harris" (1994, 58).

As the voices of this volume suggest, women filmmakers of the African and Asian disapora are working toward opening up spaces of intervention and agency, reclaiming subjective identity-making processes, and retrieving repressed histories. The women who works are explored in this volume are just a few of the many new voices who are challenging the conventional politics of representation within the cinema as it is configured today. With each new effort, these women are exploring themes of self- actualization, re-visualization, and the reclamation of history, to create an exciting and vibrantly new visual culture that speaks from the heart of the African and Asian diaspora. More women will undoubtedly come forward in the future of cinema and video to create new and challenging works, just as these women are building upon the works of those women filmmakers who came before them. But each artist discussed within this volume has left her unique imprint on the visual culture of the cinema/video apparatus, and questioned many of the assumptions that underlie our conventional appreciation of the cinema. Their work is to be encouraged, supported, and screened as widely as possible. Only when their visions are fully appreciated for the revolutionary visions that they truly are will we be closer to some sort of egalitarian instinct within the boundaries of cinema/video discourse, a discourse that is increasing in intensity daily and transforming the ways in which we view ourselves and our shared existence.

WORKS CITED
FILM AND VIDEO RENTALS
INDEX

WORKS CITED

Abel, Elizabeth. "Black Writing, White Reading: Race and the Politics of Feminist Interpretation." *Critical Inquiry* 19.3 (Spring 1993): 470–98.

Acker, Ally. *Reel Women: Pioneers of the Cinema, 1896 to the Present.* New York: Continuum, 1993.

Adorno, Theodor W. *Aesthetic Theory.* Trans. C. Lenhardt. Ed. Gretel Adorno and Rolf Tiedemann. London: Routledge, 1983.

Albrecht, Lisa, and Rose M. Brewer, eds. *Bridges of Power: Women's Multicultural Alliances.* Philadelphia: New Society Publishers, 1990.

Alexander, Karen. "Julie Dash: *Daughters of the Dust* and a Black Aesthetic." *Women in Film: A Sight and Sound Reader.* Ed. Pam Cook and Philip Dodd. Philadelphia: Temple University Press, 1993. 224–31.

Allen, Paula Gunn. *The Sacred Hoop: Recovering the Feminine in American Indian Traditions.* Boston: Beacon Press, 1986.

Armes, Roy. *Third World Film Making and the West.* Berkeley: University of California Press, 1987.

Armstrong, David. "She doesn't like it like that." *San Francisco Examiner* 13 October 1994, 4, 7.

Arora, Poonam. "The Production of Third World Subjects for First World Consumption: *Salaam Bombay!* and *Parama.*" *Multiple Voices in Feminist Film Criticism.* Ed. Diana Carson, Linda Dittmar, and Janice Welsch. Minneapolis: University of Minnesota Press, 1994. 293–304.

Attile, Martina, and Maureen Blackwood. "Black Women and Representation: Notes from the Workshops Held in London, 1984." *Films for Women.* Ed. Charlotte Brunsdon. London: BFI, 1987. 202–8.

Baker, Houston A., Jr. "Not Without My Daughters: A Conversation with Julie Dash." *Transition: An International Review* 57 (1992): 150–66.

Bakhtin, Mikhail. *The Dialogic Imagination.* Trans. Caryl Emerson and Michael Holquist. Ed. Michael Holquist. Austin: University of Texas Press, 1981.

Ball, Ed. "*Who Killed Vincent Chin?,*" *Afterimage* 16.3 (Summer 1988): 5.

Bambara, Toni Cade. "Reading the Signs, Empowering the Eye: *Daughters of the Dust* and the Black Independent Cinema Movement." *Black American Cinema.* Ed. Manthia Diawara. New York: Routledge, 1993. 118–44.

Barker, Jennifer M. "Bodily Irruptions: The Corporeal Assault on Ethnographic Narration." *Cinema Journal* 34.3 (Spring 1995): 57–76.

Baudrillard, Jean. "The Precession of Simulacra." *Art after Modernism.* Ed. Brian Wallace. New York: New Museum of Contemporary Art, 1984. 253–82.

Bell, Diane. "Aboriginal Women, Separate Places, and Feminism." *A Reader in Feminist Knowledge.* Ed. Sneja Gunew. New York: Routledge, 1991. 13–26.

Bhabha, Homi. "The Commitment to Theory." *Questions of Third Cinema.* Ed. Jim Pines and Paul Willemen. London: BFI, 1989. 111–32.

———. "Race and the Humanities: The 'Ends' of Modernity?" *Public Culture* 4.2 (Spring 1992): 81–85.

———. *The Location of Culture.* London: Routledge, 1994.

Blau, Herbert. *Take Up the Bodies: Theatre at the Vanishing Point.* Urbana: University of Illinois Press, 1982.

Bobo, Jacqueline. *Black Women as Cultural Readers.* New York: Columbia University Press, 1995.

Bonitzer, Pascal. "The Silences of the Voice." *Narrative, Apparatus, Ideology.* Ed. Philip Rosen. New York: Columbia University Press, 1986. 319–34.

Braidotti, Rosi. *Nomadic Subjects: Embodiment and Sexual Difference in Contemporary Feminist Theory.* New York: Columbia University Press, 1994.

Branch, Shelly. "A Geechee Girl Gets Ready for the Big Time." *Emerge* (October 1990): 93–94.

Braxton, Joanne M., and Andree Nicola McLaughlin, eds. *Wild Women in the Whirlwind: Afra-American Culture and the Contemporary Literary Renaissance.* New Brunswick, NJ: Rutgers University Press, 1990. 3–21.

Brown, Georgia. "Ticket to Ride." *Village Voice* 39.21 (24 May 1994): 26.

Bruno, Giuliana. *Streetwalking on a Ruined Map: Cultural Theory and the City Films of Elvira Notari.* Princeton: Princeton University Press, 1993.

Burton, Julianne. *Cinema and Social Change in America: Conversations with Filmmakers.* Austin: University of Texas Press, 1986.

———, ed. *The Social Documentary in Latin America.* Pittsburgh: University of Pittsburgh Press, 1990.

Butler, Judith. *Gender Trouble.* New York: Routledge, 1990.

Campbell, Loretta. "Reinventing Our Image: Eleven Black Women Filmmakers." *Heresies* 4.4 (1983): 58–62.

Carby, Hazel. "White Woman Listen! Black Feminism and the Boundaries of Sisterhood." *The Empire Strikes Back: Race and Racism in 70s Britain.* Ed. Centre for Contemporary Cultural Studies. London: Hutchinson, 1982. 212–35.

Carr, Robert. "Crossing the First World/Third World Divides: Testimonial, Transnational Feminisms, and the Postmodern Condition." *Scattered Hegemonies: Postmodernity and Transnational Feminist Practices.* Ed. Inderwal Grewal and Caren Kaplan. Minneapolis: University of Minnesota Press, 1994, 153–72.

Chamberlain, Joy, and Isaac Julien, Stuart Marshall, and Pratibha Parmar. "Filling the Lack in Everyone is Quite Hard Work, Really . . . A Round Table Discussion with Joy Chamberlain, Isaac Julien, Stuart Marshall, and Pratibha Parmar." *Queer Looks: Perspectives on Lesbian and Gay Film and Video.* Ed. Martha Gever, John Greyson, and Pratibha Parmar. New York: Routledge, 1993. 41–60.

Chambers, Veronica. "Finally, A Black Woman Behind the Camera." *Glamour* (March 1992): 111.

Chen, Nancy N., and Trinh T. Minh-ha. "Speaking Nearby." *Visualizing Theory*. Ed. Lucien Taylor. New York: Routledge, 1994. 432–51.

Cheuk-to, Li. "The Return of the Father: Hong Kong New Wave and Its Chinese Context in the 1980s." *New Chinese Cinemas: Forms, Identities, Politics*. Ed. Nick Brown, Paul G. Pickowicz, Vivian Sobchack, and Esther Yau. Cambridge: Cambridge University Press, 1994.

Choy, Christine. "Interview: Women in the Director's Chair." *Profile: Video Data Bank* 5.1. Chicago: Art Institute of Chicago, 1985.

Christian, Barbara. "Trajectories of Self-Definition: Placing Contemporary Afro-American Women's Fiction." *Conjuring: Black Women, Fiction and Literary Tradition*. Ed. Marjorie Pryse and Hortense J. Spillers. Bloomington: Indiana University Press, 1985. 223–48.

Chua, Lawrence. "Beach Blanket Britain." *Village Voice* 39.22 (31 May 1994): 62.

Clifford, James. *The Predicament of Culture: Twentieth Century Ethnography, Literature and Art*. Cambridge: Harvard University Press, 1988.

Code, Lorraine. *Rhetorical Spaces: Essays on Gendered Locations*. New York: Routledge, 1995.

Cohan, Charly. "*Who Killed Vincent Chin?*" *Cineaste* 17.1 (1989): 20.

Cole, Janis, and Holly Dale, eds. *Calling the Shots: Profiles of Women Filmmakers*. Kingston, Ontario: Quarry Press, 1993.

Collins, Patricia Hill. "The Social Construction of Black Feminist Thought." *Signs* 14.4 (1989): 1–30.

———. *Black Feminist Thought: Knowledge, Consciousness and the Politics of Empowerment*. London: HarperCollins, 1990.

Coronil, Fernando. "Can Postcoloniality be Decolonized? Imperial Banality and Postcolonial Power." *Public Culture* 5.1 (Fall 1992): 89–108.

Cripps, Thomas. *Slow Fade to Black: The Negro in American Film, 1900–1942*. New York: Oxford University Press, 1977.

———. *Black Film as Genre*. Bloomington: Indiana University Press, 1978.

Cruz, Robert. "Black Cinema, Film Theory and Dependent Knowledge." *Screen* 26 (May–August 1985): 3–4.

Daly, Ann. "Dance History and Feminist Theory: Reconsidering Isadora Duncan and the Male Gaze." *Gender and Performance*. Ed. Laurence Senelick. Hanover, NH: Tufts University Press, 1992. 239–59.

Dash, Julie. *Daughters of the Dust: The Making of an African American Woman's Film*. New York: New Press, 1992.

Davis, Angela. *Women, Race and Class*. New York: Random House, 1983.

Davis, R. C. "Cixous, Spivak, and Oppositional Theory." *Literature Interpretation Theory* 4.1 (1992): 29–42.

Davis, Zeinabu irene. "An Interview with Julie Dash." *Wide Angle* 13: 3/4 (July–October 1991): 110–18.

Day, Barbara. "Black Woman Makes 'the kind of film I've always wanted to see.'" *Guardian* (22 January 1992): 19–20.

de Certeau, Michel. *The Practice of Everyday Life*. Berkeley: University of California Press, 1980.

de Lauretis, Teresa. *Technologies of Gender*. Bloomington: Indiana University Press, 1987.

———. *The Practice of Love: Lesbian Sexuality and Perverse Desire*. Bloomington: Indiana University Press, 1994.

———. "Rethinking Women's Cinema." *Multiple Voices in Feminist Film Criticism*. Ed. Diane Carson, Linda Dittmar, and Janice R. Welsch. Minneapolis: University of Minnesota Press, 1994: 140–61.

———, ed. *Feminist Studies/Critical Studies*. Bloomington: Indiana University Press, 1986.

Deleuze, Gilles. *Cinema 1: The Movement Image*. Trans. Hugh Tomlinson and Barbara Habberjam. Minneapolis: University of Minnesota Press, 1986.

Deleuze, Gilles, and Félix Guattari. *A Thousand Plateaus: Capitalism and Schizophrenia*. Trans. Brian Massumi. Minneapolis: University of Minnesota Press, 1987.

De Marinis, Marco. *The Semiotics of Performance*. Trans. Aine O'Healy. Bloomington: Indiana University Press, 1993.

Derrida, Jacques. *The Ear of the Other*. Trans. Peggy Kamuf. Ed. Christie McDonald. Lincoln: University of Nebraska Press, 1985.

Dharwadker, Aparna. "Historical Fictions and Postcolonial Representation: Reading Girish Karnad's *Tughlaq*." *PMLA* 110.1 (January 1995): 43–58.

Diawara, Manthia. *African Cinema: Politics and Culture*. Bloomington: Indiana University Press, 1992.

———, ed. *Black American Cinema*. New York: Routledge, 1993.

Dittus, Erick. "Mississippi Triangle: An Interview with Christine Choy, Worth Long and Allan Siegel." *Cineaste* 14. 2 (1985): 38–40.

Dixon, Wheeler Winston. *It Looks At You: The Returned Gaze of Cinema*. Albany: State University of New York Press, 1995.

Doane, Mary Ann. "The Voice in the Cinema: The Articulation of Body and Space." *Narrative, Apparatus, Ideology*. ed. Philip Rosen. New York: Columbia University Press, 1986. 335–48.

———. *The Desire to Desire*. Bloomington: Indiana University Press, 1987.

———. "Dark Continents: Epistemologies of Racial and Sexual Difference." *Femmes Fatales*. Ed. Mary Ann Doane. New York: Routledge, 1991. 209–48.

Erikson, Joan. *Mata ni Pachedi: A Book on the Temple Cloth of the Mother Goddess*. Ahmedabad, India: National Institute of Design, 1968.

Everett, Anna. "The Other Pleasures: The Narrative Function of Race in the Cinema." *Film Criticism* 20.1/2 (Fall/Winter 1995–96): 26–38.

Felman, Shoshana. "Turning the Screw of Interpretation." *Literature and Psychoanalysis*. Ed. Shoshana Felman. Baltimore: Johns Hopkins University Press, 1980. 94–207.

Filemyr, Ann. "Zeinabu irene Davis: Filmmaker, Teacher with a Powerful Mission." *Angles* 1.2 (Winter 1992): 6–9, 22.

Flax, Jane. *Disputed Subjects: Essays on Psychoanalysis, Politics and Philosophy*. New York: Routledge, 1993.

Foster, Frances Smith. *Written by Herself*. Bloomington: Indiana University Press, 1993.

Foster, Gwendolyn Audrey. Interview with Zeinabu irene Davis. July 1995.

Foster, Thomas. "Circles of Oppression, Circles of Repression: Etel Adnan's *Sitt Marie Rose*." *PMLA* 110.1 (January 1995): 59–74.

Foucault, Michel. *Discipline and Punish*. Trans. Alan Sheridan. New York: Vintage, 1979.

Fraleigh, Sondra Horton. *Dance and the Lived Body*. Pittsburgh: University of Pittsburgh Press, 1987.

Freedman, Samuel G. "One People in Two Worlds." *New York Times* 2 February 1992, 13–14.

Friedberg, Anne. "A Denial of Difference: Theories of Cinematic Identification." *Psychoanalysis and Cinema*. Ed. E. Ann Kaplan. New York: Routledge, 1990, 36–45.

Fusco, Coco. "Sankofa and Black Audio Film Collective," *Discourses: Conversations in Post Modern Art and Culture*. Ed. Russell Ferguson, William Olander, Karen Fiss, and Marcia Tucker. Cambridge: Massachusetts Institute of Technology and New Museum of Contemporary Art, 1990. 17–43.

Gabriel, Teshome H. "Thoughts on Nomadic Aesthetics and the Black Independent Cinema: Traces of a Journey." *Blackframes*. Ed. Mbye B. Cham and Claire Andrade-Watkins. Cambridge: MIT Press, 1988. 62–79.

——. "Third Cinema as Guardian of Popular Memory: Towards a Third Aesthetics." *Questions of Third Cinema*. Ed. Jim Pines and Paul Willemen. London: BFI, 1989. 53–64.

Gaines, Jane. "White Privilege and Looking Relationships." *Issues in Feminist Film Criticism*. Ed. Patricia Erens. Bloomington: Indiana University Press, 1990. 197–214.

Gates, Henry Louis. "Looking for Modernism." *Black American Cinema*. Ed. Manthia Diawara. New York: Routledge, 1993. 200–207.

Gibbs, James Lowell, Jr. "*Daughters of the Dust*." *African Arts* 26 (January 1993): 81–83.

Gibson, Gloria. "Aspects of Black Feminist Cultural Ideology in Films by Black Women Artists." *Multiple Voices in Feminist Film Criticism*. Ed. Diane Carson, Linda Dittmar, and Janice R. Welsch. Minneapolis: University of Minnesota Press, 1994. 365–79.

Gilroy, Paul. "Police and Thieves." *The Empire Strikes Back: Race and Racism in 70s Britain*. Ed. Centre for Contemporary Cultural Studies. London: Hutchinson, 1982. 143–82.

Golden, Tim. "*Danzón* Glides to a Soft Mexican Rhythm." *New York Times* 11 October 1992, 24.

Goldman, Debra. "*Who Killed Vincent Chin?*" *American Film* 13. 8 (May 1988): 8.

Gordon, Linda. "On 'Difference.' " *Genders* 10 (Spring 1991): 91–111.

Gossage, Leslie. "Black Women Independent Filmmakers: Changing Images of Black Women." *Iris* (Spring–Summer 1987): 4–11.

Greenblatt, Stephen. "Introduction: New World Encounters." *New World Encounters*. Ed. Stephen Greenblatt. Berkeley: University of California Press, 1993. vii–xvii.

Grosz, Elizabeth. *Volatile Bodies: Toward a Corporeal Feminism*. Bloomington: Indiana University Press, 1994.

Guerrero, Ed. "The Black Image in Protective Custody: Hollywood's Biracial Buddy Films of the Eighties." *Black American Cinema*. Ed. Manthia Diawara. New York: Routledge, 1993. 237–46.

Hall, Stuart. "Encoding, Decoding." *The Cultural Studies Reader*. Ed. Simon During. London: Routledge, 1993. 90–103.

Hanna, Judith Lynne. *The Performer-Audience Connection: Emotion to Metaphor in Dance and Society*. Austin: University of Texas Press, 1983.

Hanson, Peter. "NYU Professor's Journey into Film." *Washington Square News* 29 March 1989, 5, 17.

Hart, Trevor Ray. "The Brit Pack." *Time Out* (23 March 1994): 18–22.

Harvey, Sylvia. "Third World Perspectives: Focus on Sarah Maldoror." *Women and Film* 1. 5/6 (1974): 71–75, 110.

Hoffman, Jan. "Mom Always Said, Don't Take the First $2 Million Offer." *New York Times* 9 October 1994, 28.

hooks, bell. "Black Women Filmmakers Break the Silence." *Black Film Review* 2.3 (Summer 1986): 14–15.

———. *Black Looks: Race and Representation*. Boston: South End Press, 1992.

———. "The Oppositional Gaze: Black Female Spectators." *Black American Cinema*. Ed. Manthia Diawara. New York: Routledge, 1993. 288–302.

———. "A Call for Militant Resistance." *Multiple Voices in Feminist Film Criticism*. Ed. Diane Carson, Linda Dittmar, and Janice R. Welsch. Minneapolis: University of Minnesota Press, 1994. 358–79.

———. "Save Your Breath Sisters." *New York Times* 17 January 1996, 19.

Hornaday, Ann. "In *Bhaji on the Beach*, Feminism Meets the Diaspora." *New York Times* 22 May 1994, 29.

Jablonko, Allison. "New Guinea in Italy: An Analysis of the Making of Italian Television Series from Research Footage of the Maring People of Papua, New Guinea." *Anthropological Filmmaking*. Ed. J. Rollwagon. Chur: Harwood Publishers, 1988. 169–96.

Jackson, Devon. "As She Likes It." *Village Voice* 18 October 1994, 58.

———. "Who's Zooming What." *Village Voice* Special Film Section 21 May 1996, 15.

Jackson, Elizabeth. "Barbara McCullough: Independent Filmmaker." *Jump Cut* 36 (1990): 94–97.

Jackson, Lynn, and Jean Rasenberger. "An Interview with Martina Attile and Isaac Julien." *Cineaste* 14.4 (1988): 23–37.

Jaehne, Karen. "Boat People: In Interview with Ann Hui." *Cineaste* 13.2 (1984): 16–19.

Jameson, Fredric. "Imaginary and Symbolic in Lacan: Marxism, Psychoanalytic Criticism, and the Problem of the Subject." *Literature and Psychoanalysis*. Ed. Shoshana Felman. Baltimore: Johns Hopkins University Press, 1980. 338–95.

Jones, Anderson. "Black Female Director Focuses on Relationships." *Detroit Free Press* 14 October 1994, 1, 12.

Jones, Lynda. "Dream On, Dreamer." *Village Voice* 6 September 1994, 60.

Jordan, June. *Technical Difficulties: African-American Notes on the State of the Union*. New York: Pantheon, 1992.

Jules-Rossette, Bennetta. *The Messages of Tourist Art: An African Semiotic System in Comparative Perspective*. New York: Plenum, 1984.

Julien, Isaac, and Kobena Mercer. "De Margin and De Centre." *Screen* 29.4 (Autumn 1988): 2–10.

Kafi-Akua, Afua. "Ayoka Chenzira: Filmmaker." *Sage* 4.1 (Spring 1987): 69–72.

Kaplan, Caren. "The Politics of Location as Transnational Feminist Critical Practice." *Scattered Hegemonies: Postmodernity and Transnational Feminist Practices.* Ed. Inderwal Grewel and Caren Kaplan. Minneapolis: University of Minnesota Press, 1994. 137–52.

Kaplan, David A. "Film About a Beating Examines a Community." *New York Times* 16 July 1989, 27.

Kaplan, E. Ann. "Problematizing Cross-Cultural Analysis: The Case of Women in the Recent Chinese Cinema." *Wide Angle* 11. 2 (1989): 40–50.

Khush Collective. "Fighting Back: An Interview with Pratibha Parmar." *A Lotus of Another Color: An Unfolding of the South Asian Gay and Lesbian Experience.* Ed. Rakesh Ratti. Boston: Alyson, 1993. 34–40.

Klostermaier, Klaus K. "Sakti: Hindu Images and Concepts of the Goddess." *Goddesses in Religion and Modern Debate.* Ed. Larry W. Hurtado. Atlanta: Scholars Press, 1990. 143–61.

Kristeva, Julia. *Revolution in Poetic Language.* Trans. Margaret Waller. New York: Columbia University Press, 1984.

Kruger, Barbara. "Sankofa Film/Video Collective and Black Audio Film Collective [at] The Collective For Living Cinema." *Artforum* (September 1988): 143–44.

Larkin, Alile Sharon. "Black Women Film-Makers Defining Ourselves: Feminism in Our Own Voice." *Female Spectators.* Ed. E. Deidre Pribram. London: Verso, 1988. 157–73.

Lekatsas, Barbara. "Encounters: The Film Odyssey of Camille Billops." *Black American Literature Forum* 25. 2 (Summer 1991): 395–408.

Lindsey, Beverly, ed. *Comparative Perspectives on Third World Women: The Impact of Race, Sex, and Class.* New York: Praeger, 1980.

Longley, Kateryna Olijnyk. "Autobiographical Storytelling by Australian Aboriginal Women." *De/Colonizing the Subject: The Politics of Gender in Women's Autobiography.* Ed. Sidonie Smith and Julie Watson. Minneapolis: University of Minnesota Press, 1992. 370–84.

López, Ana. "Tears and Desire: Women and Melodrama in the 'Old' Mexican Cinema." *Multiple Voices in Feminist Film Criticism.* Minneapolis: University of Minnesota Press, 1994. 254–70.

Lutz, Catherine A. and Jane L. Collins. *Reading National Geographic.* Chicago: University of Chicago Press, 1993.

Lyotard, Jean François. *The Postmodern Condition: A Report on Knowledge.* Minneapolis: University of Minnesota Press, 1991.

MacDougall, David. "Whose Story Is It?" *Visualizing Theory.* Ed. Lucien Taylor, New York: Routledge, 1994a. 27–36.

MacDougall, David. "Films of Memory." *Visualizing Theory.* Ed. Lucien Taylor, New York: Routledge, 1994b. 260–70.

Martin, Angela. "Four Filmmakers from West Africa." *Framework* 11 (1979): 16–21.

Martin, Michael T., ed. *Cinemas of the Black Diaspora*. Detroit: Wayne State University Press, 1995.

Maslin, Janet. "A Bronx Charmer with Problems and All the Answers." *New York Times* 14 October 1994, 15.

Mayne, Judith. *The Woman at the Keyhole: Feminism and Women's Cinema*. Bloomington: Indiana University Press, 1990.

———. *Cinema and Spectatorship*. New York: Routledge, 1993.

———. "A Parallax View of Lesbian Authorship." *Feminisms in the Cinema*. ed. Laura Pietropaolo and Ada Testaferri. Bloomington: Indiana University Press, 1995. 195–205.

Mellencamp, Patricia. "Making History: Julie Dash." *Frontiers* 15.1 (1994): 76–101.

Mercer, Kobena. *Welcome to the Jungle: New Positions in Black Cultural Studies*. New York: Routledge, 1994.

Minh-ha, Trinh T. *Woman, Native, Other: Writing Postcoloniality and Feminism*. Bloomington: Indiana University Press, 1989

———. *When the Moon Waxes Red: Representation, Gender, and Cultural Politics*. New York: Routledge, 1991.

———. *Framer Framed*. New York: Routledge, 1992.

———. "*A Tale of Love* Press Packet." New York: Women Make Movies, 1995.

Modleski, Tania. "Feminism and the Power of Interpretation: Some Critical Readings." *Feminist Studies/Critical Studies*. Ed. Teresa de Lauretis. Bloomington: Indiana University Press, 1986. 121–38.

Mohanty, Chandra Talpade. "Under Western Eyes: Feminist Scholarship and Colonial Discourses." *Third World Women and the Politics of Feminism*. Ed. Chandra Talpade Mohanty, Ann Russo, and Lourdes Torres. Bloomington: Indiana University Press, 1991. 51–80.

Moore, Henrietta L. *Space, Text, and Gender: An Anthropological Study of the Marakwet of Kenya*. Cambridge: Cambridge University Press, 1986.

Morrison, Toni. *Playing in the Dark: Whiteness in the Literary Imagination*. New York: Knopf, 1992.

Naficy, Hamid. "Exile Discourses and Televisual Fetishization." *Quarterly Review of Film and Video* 13. 1–3 (1991): 85–116.

Nair, Mira. "*India Cabaret*: Reflections and Reactions." *Discourse* 8 (Fall–Winter 1986/7): 58–72.

Nichols, Bill. *Blurred Boundaries*. Bloomington: Indiana University Press, 1994.

Nicholson, David. "Independent—and Liking It." *American Visions* (July–August 1986a): 55.

———. "Conflict and Complexity: Filmmaker Kathleen Collins." *Black Film Review* 2. 3 (Summer 1986b): 16–17.

Okazawa-Rey, Margo. "Viewpoint: In Hollywood, Black Men Are In; Black Women Are Still Out." *Black Film Review* 6.1 (1990–91): 25.

Parmar, Pratibha. "That Moment of Emergence." *Queer Looks: Perspectives on Lesbian and Gay Film and Video*. Ed. Pratibha Parmar, John Greyson, and Martha Gever. New York: Routledge, 1993. 3–11.

Pearlman, Cindy. "Fame Hasn't Found Her—Yet: Hot Director Darnell Martin Isn't Interested in Spotlight." *Sacramento Bee* 9 October 1994, 11–12.

Pfaff, Françoise. *Twenty-Five Black African Filmmakers: A Critical Study with Filmography and Biobibliography*. Westport CT: Greenwood Press, 1988.

Phillips, Julie. "Growing Up Black and Female: Leslie Harris's *Just Another Girl on the I.R.T.*" *Cineaste* 19. 4 (1992): 86–87.

Pines, Jim. "*The Passion of Remembrance*: Interview with Sankofa Film Collective. *Framework* 32/33 (1986): 92–99.

Pines, Jim and Paul Willemen, ed. *Questions of Third Cinema*. London: BFI, 1989.

Pintchman, Tracy. *The Rise of the Goddess in the Hindu Tradition*. Albany: State University of New York Press, 1994.

Pribram, Deidre E., ed. *Female Spectators: Looking at Film and Television*. London: Verso, 1988.

Pryse, Marjorie, and Hortense Spillers, ed. *Conjuring: Black Women, Fiction, and Literary Tradition*. Bloomington: Indiana University Press, 1985.

Rattigan, Neil. *Images of Australia*. Dallas: Southern Methodist University Press, 1991.

Reid, Mark. "Rebirth of a Nation." *Southern Exposure* 20.4 (Winter 1992): 26–28.

———. *Redefining Black Film*. Berkeley: University of California Press, 1993.

Ringel, Eleanor. "Husbands and Wives in the 'Hood.' " *Atlanta Journal* 14 October 1994, 32.

Rodman, Howard A. "Between Black and White." *Elle* (October 1989): 132.

Rosaldo, Renato. *Culture and Truth: The Remaking of Social Analysis*. Boston: Beacon Press, 1993a.

———. "After Objectivism." *The Cultural Studies Reader*. Ed. Simon During. London: Routledge, 1993b. 104–17.

Said, Edward. *Culture and Imperialism*. New York: Knopf, 1993.

Sandoval, Chela. "US Third World Feminism: The Theory and Method of Oppositional Consciousness in the Postmodern World." *Genders* 10 (Spring 1991): 1–24.

Scarry, Elaine. *The Body in Pain*. New York: Oxford University Press, 1985.

Schechner, Richard. *Between Theater & Anthropology*. Philadelphia: University of Pennsylvania Press, 1985.

———. *Performance Theory*. New York: Routledge, 1988.

Schissel, Howard. "Africa on Film: The First Feminist View." *Guardian* 9 July 1980, 7.

Schneman, Naomi. *Engenderings: Constructions of Knowledge, Authority and Privilege*. New York: Routledge, 1993.

Schott, Robin May. "Rereading the Canon: Kantian Purity and the Suppression of Eros." *Modern Engendering: Critical Feminist Readings in Modern Western Philosophy*. Ed. Bat-Ami Bar On. Albany: State University of New York Press, 1994. 127–39.

Seremetakis, C. Nadia. "The Memory of the Senses, Historical Perception, Commensal Exchange, and Modernity." *Visualizing Theory*. Ed. Lucien Taylor. New York: Routledge, 1994: 214–29.

Shah, Amit. "A Dweller in Two Lands: Mira Nair, Filmmaker." *Cineaste* 15.3 (1987), 22–24.

Shah, Nayan. "Sexuality, Identity, and the Uses of History." *A Lotus of Another Color: An Unfolding of the South Asian Gay and Lesbian Experience*. Ed. Ratti Rakesh. Boston: Alyson, 1993, 113–32.

Sharpe, Jenny. *Allegories of Empire: The Figure of Woman in the Colonial Text*. Minneapolis: University of Minnesota Press, 1993.

Shaviro, Steven. *The Cinematic Body*. Minneapolis: University of Minnesota Press, 1993.

Shen, Ted. "Reel Life: New Lessons from African Folklore." *Chicago Reader* 24.40 (7 July 1995): 6.

Sherman, Charlotte Watson. "Introduction." *Sisterfire: Black Womanist Fiction and Poetry*. Ed. Charlotte Watson Sherman. New York: HarperCollins, 1994. xv–xix.

Silverman, Kaja. "Suture [Excerpts]." *Narrative, Apparatus, Ideology*. Ed. Philip Rosen. New York: Columbia University Press, 1986. 219–35.

Smith, Sidonie, and Julia Watson. Introduction. *De/Colonizing the Subject: The Politics of Gender in Women's Autobiography*. Ed. Sidonie Smith and Julia Watson. Minneapolis: University of Minnesota Press, 1992. xi–xxxi.

Smith, Valerie. "Reconstituting the Image: The Emergent Black Woman Director." *Callaloo* 11. 4 (Fall 1988): 710–19.

Snead, James. "Recoding Blackness: The Visual Rhetoric of Black Independent Film." *Circular for the New American Filmmakers Series* 23. 1/2 New York: Whitney Museum of American Art, 1985.

Sobchack, Vivian. *The Address of the Eye: A Phenomenology of Film Experience*. Princeton: Princeton University Press, 1992.

Spivak, Gayatri Chakravorty. *In Other Worlds: Essays in Cultural Politics*. New York: Methuen, 1987.

——. "Can the Subaltern Speak?" *Marxism and the Interpretation of Culture*. Ed. Cary Nelson and Lawrence Grossberg. Urbana: University of Illinois Press, 1988. 217–313.

——. "Acting Bits/Identity Talk," *Critical Inquiry* 18. 4 (Summer 1992): 770–803.

Springer, Claudia. "Black Women Filmmakers." *Jump Cut* 29 (1984): 34–37.

Stoller, Paul. "Artaud, Rouch and the Cinema of Cruelty." *Visualizing Theory*. ed. Lucien Taylor. New York: Routledge, 1994. 84–98.

Straayer, Chris. "The Hypothetical Lesbian Heroine." *Multiple Voices in Feminist Film Criticism*. Ed. Diane Carson, Linda Dittmar and Janice R. Welsch. Minneapolis: University of Minnesota Press, 1994. 343–57.

Stuart, Andrea. "Mira Nair: A New Hybrid Cinema," *Women and Film: A Sight and Sound Reader*. Pam Cook and Philip Dodd, eds. Philadelphia: Temple University Press, 1993. 210–16.

Suleiman, Susan Rubin. *Risking Who One Is: Encounters with Contemporary Art and Literature*. Cambridge: Harvard University Press, 1994.

Suleri, Sara. "Woman Skin Deep: Feminism and the Postcolonial Condition." *Critical Inquiry* 18.4 (Summer 1992): 756–69.

Sumner, Jane. "Sassy Saga from the Barrio." *Dallas Morning News* 26 October 1994, 1–2.

Tate, Greg. "Cinematic Sisterhood." *Village Voice* 4 June 1991, 77–78.

———. "La Vénus Nègre." *Artforum* 30.1 (January 1992): 90–93.

———. "Just Another Girl: Flygirl on Film." *Village Voice* 23 March 1993, 58.

Taubin, Amy. "Art and Industry." *Village Voice* 26 November 1991, 66.

———. "Working Girls." *Village Voice* 24 November 1992, 68.

Taylor, Clyde. "Shooting the Black Woman." *Black Collegian* 9 (May–June, 1979): 94–96.

———. "Storming the Gates of Freedom: Three Films on Black Women." *Black Collegian* 12 (April–May, 1982): 26.

———. "The LA Rebellion: New Spirit in American Film." *Black Film Review* 2.2 (1986): 29.

———. "The Paradox of Black Independent Film." *Black Film Review* 4. 4 (Fall 1988): 2–3, 17–19.

———. "The Birth of Black Cinema: An Overview." *Black International Cinema* 1. 5 (February 1989): 115–17.

———. "Doing the Right Thing." *Art Forum International* (October 1989): 20–22.

———. "The Future of Black Film: The Debate Continues." *Black Film Review* 5.3 (1990): 7, 9, 27–28.

Third World Newsreel, *Third World Newsreel Catalogue.* New York: Third World Newsreel, 1995.

Thomas, Kevin. "Salute Set for Black Women in Film." *Los Angeles Times* 29 January 1982, 15.

Thompson, Felix, "Metaphors of space: Polarization, Dualism and Third World Cinema." *Screen* 34.1 (Spring 1993): 38–53.

Thompson, Gary. "The Bronx, with Some Cheer." *Philadelphia Daily News* 14 October 1994, 43.

Treut, Monika. "Female Misbehavior." *Feminisms in the Cinema.* Ed. Laura Pietropaolo and Ada Testaferri. Bloomington: Indiana University Press, 1995. 106–21.

Ukadike, N. Frank. "Reclaiming Images of Women in Films From Africa and the Black Diaspora." *Frontiers* 15.1 (1994): 102–86.

Vernet, Marc. "The Look at the Camera." *Cinema Journal* 28.2 (Winter 1989): 48–63.

Wang, Yeujin. "The Cinematic Other and the Cultural Self? De-centering the Cultural Identity on Cinema." *Wide Angle* 11.2 (May 1989): 32–39.

Walker, Alice. *Possessing the Secret of Joy.* New York: Harcourt Brace Jovanovich, 1992.

Walker, Alice, and Pratibha Parmar. *Warrior Marks: Female Genital Mutilation and the Sexual Binding of Women.* New York: Harcourt Brace Jovanovich, 1993.

Wallace, Michele. *Invisibility Blues: From Pop to Theory.* London: Verso, 1990.

———. "Race, Gender and Psychoanalysis in Forties Film: Lost Boundaries, Home of the Brave and The Quiet One." *Black American Cinema.* Ed. Manthia Diawara. New York: Routledge, 1993. 257–71.

Welsch, Janice R. "Bakhtin, Language, and Women's Documentary Filmmaking." *Multiple Voices in Feminist Film Criticism.* Ed. Diane Carson, Linda Dittmar, and Janice R. Welsch. Minneapolis: University of Minnesota Press, 1994. 162–75.

West, Cornel. "The New Cultural Politics of Difference." *The Cultural Studies Reader.* Ed. Simon During,. London: Routledge, 1993: 203–17.

Willemen, Paul. "Letter to John." *Screen* 21.2 (Summer 1980): 53–66.

Wilmington, Mike. "Euzhan Palcy: For All the Black Shack Alleys." *Los Angeles Weekly* 11 May 1984, 24.

Women Make Movies. *Women Make Movies Catalog.* New York: Women Make Movies, 1995.

Yearwood, Gladstone L. *Black Cinema Aesthetics: Issues in Independent Black Filmmaking.* Athens: Ohio University Center for Afro-American Studies, 1982.

Zarrilli, Phillip B. "What Does it Mean to 'Become the Character': Power, Presence, and Transcendence in Asian In-body Disciplines of Practice." *By Means of Performance: Intercultural Studies of Theatre and Ritual.* Ed. Richard Schechner and Willa Appel. Cambridge: Cambridge University Press, 1990: 131–48

Zavarzadeh, Mas'ud. *Seeing Films Politically.* Albany: State University of New York Press, 1991.

FILM AND VIDEO RENTALS

Most of the films discussed in this volume may be rented or purchased in 16mm or video format from:

Women Make Movies, Inc.
462 Broadway, Suite 500D
New York, NY 10013
PHONE (212) 925 0606
FAX (212) 925 2052
E-mail: distdept@wmm.com

Third World Newsreel
335 West 38th Street, 5th floor
New York, New York 10018
PHONE (212) 947 9277
FAX (212) 549 6417

Crosscurrent Media/National Asian American
Telecommunications Association
346 Ninth Street, 2nd floor
San Francisco, CA 94103

INDEX

Gwendolyn Audrey Foster is an assistant professor of English at the University of Nebraska, specializing in film and cultural studies. Foster is the author of *Women Film Directors: An International Bio-Critical Dictionary*. Her forthcoming books include an anthology of criticism on filmmaker Chantal Akerman, *Troping The Body: Gender, Etiquette, and Dialogic Performance*, and *Captive Bodies: Postcolonialist Subjectivity in the American Cinema*. Foster also wrote and directed *The Women Who Made the Movies*, a documentary on the history of women filmmakers, distributed through Women Make Movies.